Tim
Many happy
returns —

Much love.

Geraldine

Fortune Telling

Telling

A Guide to Reading the Future

Fortune Telling

A Guide to Reading the Future

Douglas Hill

Hamlyn
London New York Sydney Toronto

The Hamlyn Publishing Group wish to thank Waddingtons Playing
Card Company Limited for supplying the playing cards and the Tarot
pack used in the illustrations.

Published by
The Hamlyn Publishing Group Limited
London · New York · Sydney · Toronto
Astronaut House, Feltham, Middlesex, England

Filmset in England by Tradespools Limited, Frome, Somerset
Printed in England by Hazell, Watson & Viney Limited, Aylesbury

Contents

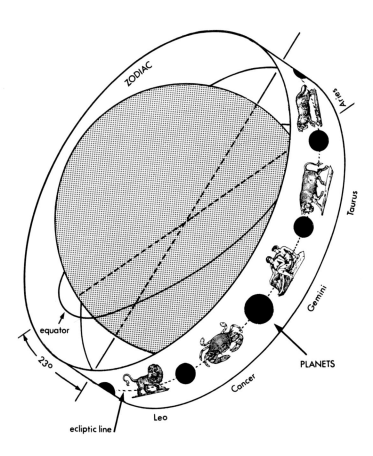

The ecliptic–the band of sky tilted at 23° to the earth's equator on which all the zodiac signs appear, and through which all ten planets seem to pass.

Fortunes
from the Far Stars

No one ever needs to make excuses for a fascination with fortune telling. It springs from the most essential part of our humanity, the part that most clearly separates us from other animals – that self-awareness which allows us to see ourselves as creatures living *within time*, able to recognise the approach of the future, able to anticipate and plan for that future. When the first hairy hominid gazed out from his cave mouth and wondered what was going to befall him next, that fascination was born. And when the first other hominid arrived at that cave mouth willing to try to answer that question, fortune telling was born.

With a pedigree so long, and so inextricably woven into our very humanity, it is no wonder that fortune telling remained of signal importance throughout human history. Today it is a multi-million-pound (and multi-national) industry commanding the attentions of the vast majority of the human race. More people today than ever before are searching for their destinies; and, while there is no shortage of specialised professionals and experts, more and more people are doing their own searching, for themselves.

That is the beauty of so many of the forms and techniques of 'divination', notably the eight or nine to be introduced in this book. They are accessible to everyone – not solely to magicians, priests, shamans, wizards and other adepts. That was not always the case with forms that were popular long ago, so today not too many people are engaged in casting runes or looking for omens in magic pools or slicing open livestock for an intestinal oracle. With today's most favoured forms, though, anyone can acquire their basic equipment, anyone can learn their basic processes and master their basic languages. In the context of the current urge towards doing it yourself and self-sufficiency, fortune telling is both easier and cheaper than, say, carpentry or dress-making, and ultimately a lot more fun. Whether it is also more rewarding will depend entirely on what you yourself make of it.

Certainly that is true of one of the oldest and most glamorous of all forms, which is also the one of which almost everyone today has some smattering (as a glance through any large-circulation newspaper or magazine will prove) – the art, established all those ages ago in ancient Babylon, of astrology. No doubt that word has instantly summoned in most readers' minds the image of their birth signs. It seems that we know our signs, and perhaps glance at our newspaper 'horoscopes', whether we are believers or scoffers. It may tell us something about how humans go on being human in spite of ours being supposedly a scientifically aware age.

Without doubt, astrology seems scientifically shaky. It seems unlikely that the position of the distant planets of this solar system, and the positions of unimaginably distant constellations of stars, could actually dictate the future of one tiny, squalling individual, as he or she makes an entrance into life on this little ball of dirt we call the earth. It seems even more unlikely when we realise that the traditions of astrology are still based on a pathetically outdated view of the solar system (the ancient notion that the earth is its centre) and on a quite erroneous idea of the actual positions of those constellations (they have moved since Babylonian times).

But all that is a familiar argument to astrologers, who are not at all traditionalists of the flat-earther type. They would probably reply that their art is *not* astronomical, that the use of planetary and stellar terminology is merely a set of 'coded symbols' for still relevant human associations. And they would perhaps quote a famous reply made by Isaac Newton to one who sneered at Newton's interest in astrology: 'I have studied it, sir; you have not.' In short, they would say, it can be seen to work.

That statement may remain open to doubt for some while yet – though none of us ought to have much respect for those who base their doubt about fortune telling on a closed-mind ignorance of the subject. The fact remains that literally millions of people believe that fortune telling works, not only because they have seen it work but because in many cases they themselves have *made* it work. As you, too, can set out to do – starting from now.

To set up as an astrologer, you need merely a pencil and paper, some simple geometric equipment, and some slim booklets to be noted later. The object is to end up with a circular chart, the horoscope, which is essentially a 'map' of where certain cosmic bodies were when the subject of the horoscope was born. But before coming to the process of drawing that map, you must first acquaint yourself with the cosmic bodies themselves – with what they spell out about the character, potentialities and destinies of people.

Path of the Sun

Though we know that the earth orbits the sun, making a complete circuit every 365 days or so, it seems to the eye that the sun orbits the earth. And as it goes along on its annual progress (we are not now talking about its *daily*, east–west 'movement'), it appears to move along a particular cosmic path. Within this path there can be seen twelve constellations, or groups of fixed stars. So the sun seems to be coinciding with the position of each constellation in turn, as the year progresses.

The path is called the zodiac; the constellations are the signs of the zodiac; and we say that the sun is 'in' one sign or another at different times of the year. The sign that the sun was in at the moment of your birth is your sun-sign or birth-sign, one of the important pieces of your personal horoscope – though not at all the only one.

Centuries of astrological scholarship have built up an immense assortment of associations and cross-references from the twelve signs to nearly every other sort of phenomenon – to, for instance, number symbolism, colours, precious stones, parts of the body, all manner of occult symbolism, other forms of fortune telling like palmistry or Tarot cards, etc. Some of this may interest you enough to pursue it elsewhere, for an expanded understanding of each sign; but space forbids its inclusion here. But this account of the zodiac cannot omit two important ways in which, traditionally, the signs are *grouped*, which can aid understanding of them.

First, there are three groupings: the *cardinal* signs (loosely, the dominant, 'active' ones, which are those that occur at the beginning of the four seasons); the *fixed* signs (more submissive, 'reactive' or indeed reactionary, sometimes termed feminine); and the *mutable* signs (neither active nor reactive but like catalysts, facilitating action, yet both changeable and resilient).

Second, there are four groupings, based on the ancient idea of the four elements – so that the signs will be each associated with one of the elements of fire, earth, air or water, and will share their traditionally characteristic qualities.

But now for more detail about the twelve individual signs themselves. (And see the illustration for the special drawn symbol for each and a ready-reference sketch of the major attributes, on pages 12–13.)

Aries. The Ram (21 March to 20 April). A cardinal sign, ushering in the spring equinox, true beginning of the year, and also a 'fire' sign. Obviously, then, full of dominating, active qualities and blazing energy – not to mention the virile aggression of its 'ram' nature. Adventurous, restless and reckless, often violent, often highly creative – a good sign for artists, explorers, pioneers of any sort, warriors, leaders and individualists.

Taurus. The Bull (21 April to 21 May). A fixed sign of earth, so tending towards the slow, cautious, earthy and even 'bovine', quite a contrast with Aries. But strong, reliable, easy-going and pleasure-loving.

Gemini. The Twins (22 May to 21 June). A mutable sign of air, so tending to be changeable to the point of being contra- dictory (the inner conflict of the 'twofold' nature). A sign of intellect and wit, articulate, given more to words than feelings – but lively and light-hearted (the 'airiness') if not all that reliable. Perhaps a lurking danger of schizophrenia, more so of egotism and pretence.

Cancer. The Crab (22 June to 22 July). The second cardinal sign, of the summer solstice, but a water sign. Strong on the intuitive and emotional side of things; sensitive, sometimes moody and insecure, often loving, always tenacious (crab- like). Sometimes called a feminine sign (and linked with

Signs of the Zodiac

Symbols	Attributes and Influences	Related Planets
♈	**Aries, the Ram.** Active, adventurous, restless, 'fiery', extraverted; a person of action, often with flair and originality, impulsive and highly sexed.	Mars
♉	**Taurus, the Bull.** Solid, reliable, 'earthy', peace-loving, pleasure-loving; perhaps slow, but neither dull nor stupid; sensual and, for women, an enhancer of femininity.	Venus
♊	**Gemini, the Twins.** Quick-witted, rational-minded, energetic, communicative; intellectual but 'airy', often changeable, with a threat of inner conflict.	Mercury
♋	**Cancer, the Crab.** Introverted, emotional, sensitive, even moody and dreamy; but loving, patient, loyal, possibly creative behind the defensive 'shell'.	Moon
♌	**Leo, the Lion.** Strong, extraverted, ambitious, dominating, energetic, essentially masculine, but more controlled and directed than Aries's activity.	Sun
♍	**Virgo, the Virgin.** Intelligent, disciplined, cool and sensible, tidy-minded and precise; a hard and often skilled worker, conscientious and devoted.	Mercury

Related Planets	Attributes and Influences	Symbols
Venus	**Libra, the Scales.** The emphasis almost entirely on balance, equilibrium; sociable, well-adjusted, peace-loving, tactful and diplomatic — often too much so.	♎
Mars (Pluto)	**Scorpio, the Scorpion.** Dark and dangerous, passionate and often aggressive, yet often able to turn this dark energy to individual, life-enhancing purposes.	♏
Jupiter	**Sagittarius, the Archer.** Outgoing, energetic, forward-looking, gregarious; lover of the outdoors and physical activity; impulsive sometimes, expansive usually.	♐
Saturn	**Capricorn, the Goat.** Independent and individualistic; cool, disciplined, perhaps a little over-cautious and gloomy; yet ambitious and probably clever and talented.	♑
Saturn (Uranus)	**Aquarius, the Water-Carrier.** Creatively artistic or scientific, spiritual, 'airy', devoted to causes like peace and brotherhood and equality among men.	♒
Jupiter (Neptune)	**Pisces, the Fish.** Idealistic, spiritual (or psychic), introverted, highly sensitive, vague and dreamy (often visionary), sometimes artistic.	♓

motherhood), but only in terms of the old view that sensitivity and intuition are exclusively female qualities.

Leo. The Lion (23 July to 23 August). Fixed sign of fire, and appropriately dominating, strong, power-seeking – as 'masculine' in the traditional stereotype as Cancer is 'feminine'. As fiery as Aries but not as impetuous: a good sign for kings, presidents and other would-be rulers, or for ambitious folk in any sphere.

Virgo. The Virgin (23 August to 23 September). Mutable sign of earth – but earthy not in the sexy sense so much as the 'feet on the ground' sense. Orderly, disciplined, neat, controlled, intelligent, perhaps finicky – a sign for scholars and craftsmen rather than for discoverers and creators.

Libra. The Scales (24 September to 23 October). The third cardinal sign (the autumn equinox), of air. Balance is of course the keyword – along with tolerance, patience, sociability. A good sign for diplomats or anyone who must get on with people; an enjoyment of culture, a humanitarian, above all a keeper of the peace. In every way the opposite of Aries' flaring tempestuousness.

Scorpio. The Scorpion (24 October to 22 November). Fixed sign of water, traditionally rather an unpleasant sign connected with dark and dangerous qualities. But also energetic, determined, self-contained, pleasure-loving, strongminded and sexy.

Sagittarius. The Archer (23 November to 21 December). A mutable sign of fire – so there are some conflicts and contradictions and also much energy. Extraverted, gregarious, adventurous, much given to the outdoors and to physical activity, a good sign for successful businessmen, sportsmen, 'achievers' of all sorts.

Capricorn. The Goat (22 December to 20 January). The fourth cardinal sign (the winter solstice), and of earth. Rather dour, inward-looking, self-sufficient, but not without cleverness and ambition. A danger of pessimism, of feelings of isolation (even paranoia), of depressive or gloomy tendencies, but lightened by its shares of common sense and conservatism.

Aquarius. The Water-Carrier (21 January to 19 February). A fixed sign of air. One of the signs of intellectual achievement and originality – unconventional, even rebellious, but humanitarian and much given to thoughts of peace and goodwill among men. A good sign for artists and creative scientists, and rebels of all sorts.

Pisces. The Fish (20 February to 20 March). Mutable sign of water, with corresponding tendencies to be, at worst, both vague and 'wet' or 'soppy'. Strong on sensitivity, idealism, imagination, sometimes psychic ability, weaker on ambition, strength of mind, stamina. Likely to be shy and introverted, a bit dreamy and unworldly (or 'other-worldly') – but capable of great love and dedication, and highly artistic once the necessary energy is found.

Rulers of the Signs

That pathway along which the sun travels from constellation to constellation happens, interestingly, to be also the strip of sky through which all the planets of our solar system can be seen to 'move'. (It is because their orbits are all more or less in the same plane.) So the moon, Mars, Venus and the

The Ten Planets

Attributes and Influences

Related signs

☉	**Sun.** Most important of the planets in a horoscope. In itself, powerful, dominating, energetic; the source of life and the vital powers; symbol of the 'masculine principle' and creativity of all sorts — like the Greco-Roman sun-god, Apollo.	Leo
☽	**Moon.** Not much less important than the sun in horoscopes. The feminine principle, concerned with inner qualities, emotions, intuitions, the irrational and so-called 'darker' elements of our being, as the goddess Diana is in her way.	Cancer
☿	**Mercury.** Intellectually clever and articulate — mentally as quick as the god but sometimes as changeable or unreliable as the metal; given more to critical analysis than creativity, but in addition to every form of communication.	Gemini Virgo
♀	**Venus.** A different sort of femininity — the 'love goddess' extremes of soft sensuality, beauty, sexuality; a gentle, easy-going, loving nature; often an element of artistry, always a strong streak of pleasure-loving.	Taurus Libra
♂	**Mars.** Masculinity taken to extremes, as befits the god of war. Extraverted, energetic activity; sometimes aggression and violence; usually courage and stamina; far more physical than intellectual, and frequently danger-loving.	Aries Scorpio

Related signs	Attributes and Influences	
Sagittarius Pisces	**Jupiter.** King of the gods and a kingly planet; expansive, dominating, ambitious, worldly; qualities of leadership and authority, of success and high achievement, both financial and in terms of social (or political) status.	♃
Capricorn Aquarius	**Saturn.** The cold, old, dark and gloomy planet (as is the god), usually a baleful influence in horoscopes; qualities of caution, chill reserve, isolation; but also hard-working, strong-minded, determined and persevering.	♄
Aquarius	**Uranus.** Qualities of progress and upheaval, reform and revolution, technological innovation, but also psychic or occult discovery; individualistic, original, impulsive, resistant to disciplines and traditions.	♅
Pisces	**Neptune.** Perhaps suitably for the god of the sea, qualities like high imagination and mysticism leading to hidden occult matters; ill-defined and imprecise in some ways, and affecting the world more than individuals.	♆
Scorpio	**Pluto.** The farthest, slowest-moving planet, gloomy, dark and dire like the god of the underworld; qualities of power-seeking, not always beneficial, persuasiveness, and hidden or secretive forms of domination.	♇

rest similarly move through the twelve signs of the zodiac, and it is of the highest importance to know what planets were 'in' which signs at the time of birth. It is also crucial to know the relationships between planets and signs, for to each sign astrology links a planet as its *ruler*. It can make all the difference to a horoscope if a planet occurs in its own sign, in a diametrically opposed sign, or whatever.

But first it is necessary to become acquainted with the planets themselves – of which the sun is treated as just another one – and their qualities, which have much in common with the signs they rule. (Again, see the illustration for the usual planetary symbols and a checklist of basic attributes, on pages 16–17.)

Sun. Most mythologies make it masculine, and astrology is no different. (Indeed, all the planets strongly resemble the old gods from whom they take their names.) Much energy, vitality, power, dominance, ambition. Ruler of Leo.

Moon. Usually a goddess, in myth, so a feminine planet – and one of the most important factors in anyone's horoscope. Linked with the emotions, intuition, the unconscious, sometimes with the occult and darker elements of the 'irrational' side of mankind. Changeable, even sometimes unstable (remember our word 'lunacy'). Ruler of Cancer.

Mercury. Clever, articulate, inventive, witty – and sometimes thought unreliable or even devious (remember another word, 'mercurial', which means unpredictable). But, equally likely, versatile and energetic, if not too involved with the emotions. Rules Gemini and Virgo.

Venus. Loving, sexy, emotional, gentle, pleasure-loving,

sometimes submissive or indecisive, and of course broadly feminine in nature. Rules Taurus and Libra.

Mars. The masculine opposite – energetic, aggressive (often hot-tempered and violent), passionate, reckless, turbulent. Ruler of Aries, of course, and Scorpio.

Jupiter. Patriarchal, dominating, powerful, extraverted, often over-expansive but also beneficial, usually convivial and pleasure-loving as well as authoritative. Ruler of Pisces and Sagittarius.

Saturn. Often said to be the most potent of all the planets, certainly the most dire and ill-favoured. Cold, gloomy, secretive, melancholic, reserved to the point of friendlessness, cautious to the point of obsession. Often associated with old age, towards which its few good points include stamina and perseverance, and wisdom. Ruler of Capricorn and, traditionally, Aquarius.

Uranus. Intelligence, some creativity, much individuality and rebelliousness. Associated with discoverers, inventors and reformers as well as with militant revolution, sometimes also with mystic and psychic matters. Since its discovery in 1781, it has been said to have taken over the rulership of Aquarius.

Neptune. Eccentricity (and sometimes that sort of brilliance or genius), emotional power (but also susceptibility), linked with mystic and darker occult matters. Discovered in 1846 and since said to have taken over the rulership of Pisces.

Pluto. Coldness and darkness, sometimes associated with death and destruction but not so much on the individual level. Discovered in 1930, said to have taken over Scorpio.

Around the Circle

Besides the sun's yearly journey along the zodiac, when it is 'in' one sign after another, the zodiac itself seems to wheel round the earth. Certainly it does so on a daily basis (as the earth spins). The horoscope acknowledges this by placing great importance on the sign that is on the eastern horizon at the moment of birth – which is called the 'rising sign' or *ascendant*.

So it is essential, in drawing a horoscope, to know not only your subject's birth date (which day of which month) but also the *time* of birth as accurately as possible (which minute of which hour). Only that allows you to calculate the ascendant accurately. And its importance can be measured by the fact that many experts take the ascendant's ruling planet as *the* most important planet in the horoscope, while others agree that it is at least as important as the ruler of the sun-sign.

Here can be seen a clear glimpse of how unsatisfactory are the newspaper astrology columns. You may very well think you are, say, a 'Taurus person' because of your birth date. But if a quite different sign was rising at your moment of birth, and if the planets tend to congregate in still other signs, Taurus will not be that much more influential, in your make-up, than these other signs. In fact very few people are 'pure' zodiac types: to be predominantly Taurus, you would need Taurus as your ascendant as well as sun-sign (which means you would have to have been born at sunrise), and perhaps a few planetary positions reinforcing Taurus as well.

And even now we have not finished with the vital parts of the horoscope. The positions of the planets also interrelate, in terms of the angles they appear to make with one another – called 'aspects' – on that circular map. (The horoscope is of course 360° just like any circle; the measurement of angles or aspects tends to be within a 10° margin of error, to allow for slight inaccuracies or imprecisions about the birth time.)

So planets are in the aspect called *conjunction* when they are within about 10° or so of one another. Two similar planets would have their like qualities reinforced by being aspected in this way; two dissimilar planets would cancel each other out. So Saturn in conjunction with Mars is a coming together of dire planets, which could spell disaster; but Venus near Mars might soften and lighten its dangers.

Planets are in *opposition* when they are about 180° apart, and opposition means clash and conflict, within the nature of the person. Jupiter in opposition to Saturn would mean that the cold and anti-social nature of the latter would constantly be undermining the ambitious and outgoing nature of the former.

Less important aspects include *square,* when planets are 90° apart, which is an unfavourable aspect – meaning that the worst, or less pleasant, qualities of the planets will have stronger influence. Also unfavourable are *semi-square* (45°) and the more obscure *sesquiquadrate* (135°) and *quincunx* (150°), though these last two are not so bad an omen as the first two.

Sextile (planets 60° apart) is a favourable aspect, as are *trine* (120°), *semisextile* (30°) and *quintile* (72°, if you wish to seek such accuracy). A *grand trine* occurs when three planets form an equal-sided triangle, and astrologers rejoice at the excellent omen in that shape.

When we come at last to the so-called *houses* of the horoscope we enter the province of the most overt pre-diction. The houses are twelve fixed and rather arbitrary divisions of the horoscope circle, starting from the point of

The Major Aspects

Effects and Influences

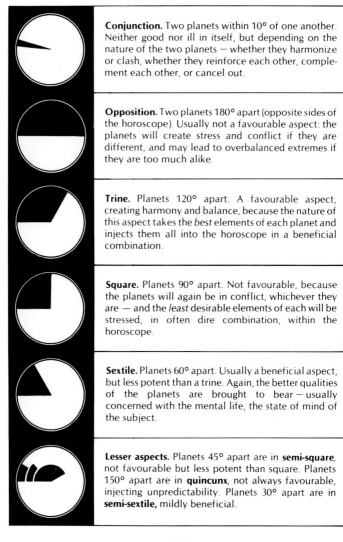

Conjunction. Two planets within 10° of one another. Neither good nor ill in itself, but depending on the nature of the two planets — whether they harmonize or clash, whether they reinforce each other, complement each other, or cancel out.

Opposition. Two planets 180° apart (opposite sides of the horoscope). Usually not a favourable aspect: the planets will create stress and conflict if they are different, and may lead to overbalanced extremes if they are too much alike.

Trine. Planets 120° apart. A favourable aspect, creating harmony and balance, because the nature of this aspect takes the *best* elements of each planet and injects them all into the horoscope in a beneficial combination.

Square. Planets 90° apart. Not favourable, because the planets will again be in conflict, whichever they are — and the *least* desirable elements of each will be stressed, in often dire combination, within the horoscope.

Sextile. Planets 60° apart. Usually a beneficial aspect, but less potent than a trine. Again, the better qualities of the planets are brought to bear — usually concerned with the mental life, the state of mind of the subject.

Lesser aspects. Planets 45° apart are in **semi-square**, not favourable but less potent than square. Planets 150° apart are in **quincunx**, not always favourable, injecting unpredictability. Planets 30° apart are in **semi-sextile,** mildly beneficial.

the ascendant. Many systems of division exist, some quite mathematically complex; but plenty of astrologers besides newcomers to the art seem to get along happily by simply dividing the circle into twelve equal pieces.

Each of the houses is an area pertaining to specific factors in the subject's life (and future) — and so it becomes vital to know how the signs and planets are placed as regards these areas. Here are the ranges of meaning for the houses:

First house: the personal self, appearance, general potentialities.

Second: wealth, possessions.

Third: siblings, education, self-expression.

Fourth: childhood, parents, family background.

Fifth: love, pleasures, recreations, children.

Sixth: health; domestic work and environment.

Seventh: marriage, business partnerships; perhaps also enemies.

Eighth: the house of death — but also inheritance.

Ninth: religious and spiritual activity, dreams and the unconscious; perhaps also travelling.

Tenth: job, occupation or career, social and community activity, reputation and status.

Eleventh: friendships; desires, ambitions, goals.

Twelfth: troubles, obstacles, limitations; enemies, secrets, betrayals; perhaps also illnesses.

The lines that separate the houses are called *cusps*, which frequently intersect zodiac signs, so that one sign may affect or relate to two houses. But these and similar interactions among all the various parts of the horoscope cannot be noted and understood until, first, the chart itself has been drawn — which process can now be begun.

The Twelve Houses

	Effects and Influences	Related signs
	First house. Relates to the personal being of the subject of a horoscope; the body and physical appearance, the essential self, outer and inner, and also the basic and most immediate life pattern.	Aries Mars
	Second house. Relates to the worldly possessions, including money and personal income; also the house of business activity, where indications will be found of success or failure, progress or setbacks, in money terms.	Taurus Venus
	Third house. Close family relationships, including siblings, aunts and uncles etc.; sometimes near neighbours; also relates to the subject's education, and to activities concerning many forms of communication.	Gemini Mercury
	Fourth house. The background of the subject — childhood home, upbringing and early life, the parents and sometimes grandparents, other family property and 'family tree' matters that affect the subject's adult life.	Cancer Moon
	Fifth house. The house of love affairs, romances, sexual relationships other than marriage; all matters concerning enjoyment, entertainment, pleasure in every sense — and places or situations where such pleasures are sought.	Leo Sun
	Sixth house. Primarily the house of health, or its absence, also relating to physical comforts, food, clothing, any aspect of the environment affecting health and comfort; and domestic surroundings — the home, even pets.	Virgo Mercury

Related signs	Effects and Influences	
Libra Venus	**Seventh house.** Relates to the marriage partner, but also to other close partner relationships, as in business; all contracts, agreements and legal commitments; hence also all dangers of treachery, disloyalty, enmity.	
Scorpio Mars	**Eighth house.** A dire house concerning losses, dangers and even death — but usually not the subject's; hence also the house of legacies and inheritances, the transfer or acquisition in this way of money or property.	
Sagittarius Jupiter	**Ninth house.** Relates to all forms of religious or spiritual activity, from churchgoing to mystic 'inner' events like visions, dreams, revelations; also the house of travelling, especially to foreign lands, often by sea.	
Capricorn Saturn	**Tenth house.** Relates to all matters involving the profession or occupation — employers or employees; promotion, achievement, rank and status; hence also outer social status, or honours, in the community and society at large.	
Aquarius Saturn (Uranus)	**Eleventh house.** The subject's close relationships with friends, companions, associates, advisers, and other important social connections; also the house of the ambitions, aims, hopes and goals in outer life.	
Pisces Jupiter (Neptune)	**Twelfth house.** Another dire house, concerning obstacles, difficulties, hardships; also including enemies, treacheries, plots against the subject; and the danger of serious restraint or failure because of these oppositions.	

Mapping the Stars

To reiterate: you need to know the day, month, year, *time* and *place* of your subject's arrival into this world. It will help your interpretation, later (and this is true of any form of fortune telling), if you also know his or her age, sex and occupation.

You will probably need to consult a good atlas (in a reference library) when it comes time to consider questions of latitude and longitude. All other questions will be answered, and essential data provided, from two other reference sources, which are in fact collections of astro-nomical fact. One is called an *ephemeris* (plural ephem-erides), usually produced year by year. The other is called a *table of houses*. They are not difficult to obtain from well-stocked scientific bookshops, from libraries or maybe through the pages of one of the many astrological magazines on newsstands. Do not be disturbed by their unfamiliarity: they will become your best friends, if you set up as an astrologer, for they do most of the work for you. All you do is perform some simple arithmetic with the data they provide.

So we begin. Let us say that your subject is a young woman who tells you that she was born on 16 September 1949 at 11.55 p.m. (That is a very accurate birth time – as accurate as most people ever can be. But any less precise, and it becomes increasingly difficult, if not impossible, to produce a horoscope.)

First step: check your ephemeris for 1949. You will find that British Summer Time operated that year until early October. So you must turn the clock back to 'sun time': her *true* birth time was 10.55 p.m. That will be our starting point: call it (A).

Second step: find the equivalent of (A) in what is called *sidereal time*. This is, roughly, time measured by stars. It is

RAPHAEL'S

ASTRONOMICAL

EPHEMERIS

OF THE

PLANETS' PLACES
for 1949

WITH TABLES OF HOUSES FOR

London, Liverpool & New York

*Containing the Longitudes of all the Planets daily and
their Latitudes and Declinations for every other
day, with the Lunar and Mutual Aspects
for every day, &c., &c.*

A COMPLETE ASPECTARIAN

MEAN TIME OBSERVED THROUGHOUT

The Tables of Houses for London are serviceable for any
place between 50° and 53° N. Latitude, the principal
cities being Antwerp, Berlin, Warsaw, Brussels, Rotterdam,
Leipzig, &c., &c.

Those for Liverpool are serviceable for Dublin, Manchester,
Sheffield, and all places between 53° and 55° N. Latitude,
including Hamburg, Danzig, Stettin, &c., &c.

Those for New York are applicable for places near the Latitude
of 40° N.; among which may be reckoned Madrid, Naples,
Rome, Istanbul, Tiflis and Pekin; and in the States—
Boston, Philadelphia, Pittsburg, Chicago, Omaha, Denver,
Salt Lake City, &c., &c.

PUBLISHED BY

Published by

W. FOULSHAM & CO., LTD.

YEOVIL ROAD   :   SLOUGH   :   BUCKS

ENGLAND.

27

slightly slower than earth time. The equivalent is found simply: you search through your ephemeris for September 1949, and among much other information there will be a column marked 'sidereal time'. Opposite 16 September you will find the figure 11.40.25. That means 11 hours 40 minutes 25 seconds (11h 40m 25s). That is our figure (B).

It represents the 'star time' equivalent of *noon* on 16 September 1949. (The ephemeris could hardly put in the sidereal time for every minute of every day of the year.) We use it to find our way to the exact sidereal-time equivalent of the subject's birth time. And we do so simply by *adding* (A)+(B): 10h 55m added to 11h 40m 25s. The result is 21h 95m 25s, which is of course 22h 35m 25s. That is our figure (C).

So far, so good. But one more small calculation is needed: a trifling compensation for the slower movement of sidereal time, to make the equivalence more exact. You must merely add to (C) an extra ten seconds for every hour after noon of the birth time. For 10.55 p.m, we must add 110 seconds (1m 50s). So we do the sum 22h 35m 25s + 1m 50s = 22h 27m 15s. That will be (D); it is also the sidereal equivalent of the birth time, and just about the most crucial figure you will have to calculate.

Now the fun can begin. But, first, to recapitulate:

You have the birth date and the time of birth.

The ephemeris tells you the sidereal time at noon on the birth date.

If the birth time is after noon, you add together the birth time and the sidereal time at noon. (Subtract the sidereal time from the birth time for forenoon births.)

You also add ten seconds per hour for every hour after noon of the birth time. (Subtract again, if forenoon.)

And you have the sidereal time of the birth time.

Now you take up your table of houses. The one you have at hand ought to be the one that corresponds with the *latitude* of the birthplace. Tables of houses for various latitudes are as easily available as ephemerides; but to make things easy, let us say that our subject was born just on the edge of London, so we want the London table of houses.

One column in the table says 'sidereal time': look down it till you come to 22 37 15. Opposite it, under the column marked 'Ascendant', you will find a rather cryptic '11.2.' Glance up the Ascendant column to find which zodiac symbol relates to this portion of the column, and you will find the sign for Cancer.

This means that the subject's 'rising sign' is Cancer, and the precise degree just on the eastern horizon at the time of birth was *11 degrees 2 minutes* (11° 2').

And now you can draw the first part of the horoscope.

Draw a good-sized circle, four inches at least in diameter. Bisect it with a horizontal line through the centre, then with a vertical line, at right angles, so the circle is quartered. The point of intersection on the left is the eastern horizon: 11° 2' Cancer, the ascendant. The point at the top is the 'mid-heaven', and the sign that falls there is fairly important too.

From the ascendant, using a simple protractor, mark off the portion of Cancer above the horizon (the horizontal line). Remember each zodiac sign covers 30 degrees (one-twelfth of a circle's 360°). So 11° of Cancer have risen above the horizon, and 19° remain below it. Mark off the upper and lower boundaries of Cancer (shown on page 31). Then, every 30°, mark off the rest of the zodiac. You then learn that the midheaven goes through Aries, and so on. You already know, from the birth date, that the sun-sign of this person is Virgo. A few things about the horoscope are already becoming clear.

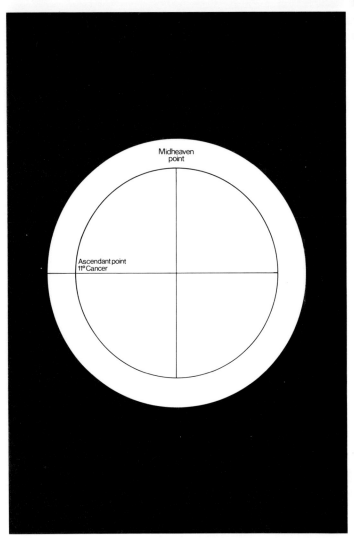

Draw a double circle and quarter it; after calculations involving sidereal time and birth time, write in the precise ascendant.

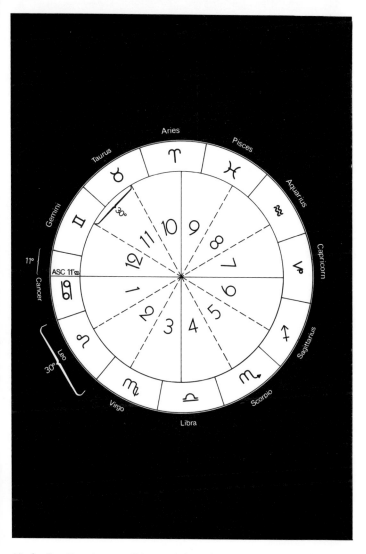

Mark off zodiac signs at 30° intervals from the upper boundary of Cancer, and the houses at 30° intervals from the ascendant point.

Time now for a digression. Our subject had the grace to be born near London, which means that her birth time was already in what is called Greenwich Mean Time. But what if she had been born outside the Greenwich time zone?

Remember that the world is divided into twenty-four time zones: when it is noon in London it is 7 a.m. in New York and 9 p.m. in Tokyo. So you must make that adjustment: translate your foreign-born subject's birth time into Greenwich Time, depending on how far ahead or behind her actual birthplace is.

Then you go on and find the 'sidereal time of birth' as we have done. But then, the tricky bit: that must be translated *back* – into the 'local' sidereal time for her actual birthplace.

There is really nothing to it. You must merely consult a good atlas and find the *longitude* of the person's birthplace. Then, for perfectly good reasons, you multiply that figure (which comes in degrees and so on) by four. That gives you a figure which you can call minutes and seconds – of *time*. (Degrees, in other words, become minutes.) And you add that to the 'sidereal time at Greenwich' of the birth – if the birthplace was east of Greenwich. Subtract if it was westwards. That little sum gives you the local sidereal time of the birth, from which you can go ahead and find the ascendant as we have already done.

End of digression: back to the horoscope of our London-born subject. You can put the houses in as the next step – merely by marking off 30° intervals starting from the ascendant point itself (see page 31). Now we are getting on well: we can see which zodiac signs are 'in' which houses, and more basic information has been gathered.

Now for the planets, for which again you rely on your ephemeris: it shows the positions on the zodiac of each planet at *noon*, again, on the day of birth.

The planets from Saturn outwards to Pluto are slow-moving, and their positions will not have altered meaningfully from noon till 10.55 (indeed, Pluto moves only about 1° a year). So their positions can be filled in right away, once you have located the right place in the tables. Look for the same area from which you looked up the sidereal time (our figure (B), earlier). Other columns in that part of the ephemeris show the planetary positions we need. So Saturn was at 11° 21′ of Virgo, Jupiter at 22° 21′ of Capricorn, and so on as shown on page 34. And some interesting things emerge right away – such as that the subject has Saturn in her sun-sign and Uranus in her rising sign.

But now it is necessary to find out exactly where the faster planets are, including the sun. And again it means a few calculations and a few searches in the ephemeris. There is no need to pause here to explain why these things are done, or what the astronomical and mathematical terms mean in this context: you may pursue such details at your leisure, in the more comprehensive textbooks. Here, you need merely to proceed with the process – using the planet Mercury (ruler of our subject's sun sign) as the example.

What you want to do is to find where Mercury was at 10.55 p.m. for our date. First, back to the ephemeris – the area you have just been using – and find where Mercury was at noon: 18° 2′ of Libra. Now turn a few pages in the ephemeris to the table showing 'planetary motions' for September. On the 16th, you find, Mercury's motion was 0° 24′.

Turn some more pages: elsewhere in the ephemeris are 'logarithm tables'. Vertical columns refer to degrees: you want the '0' column. Look down it till you intersect with the column across, referring to minutes, at 24′: the 'log' figure you get from the table is 1.7781.

Now, the vertical columns, the book says, refer to hours

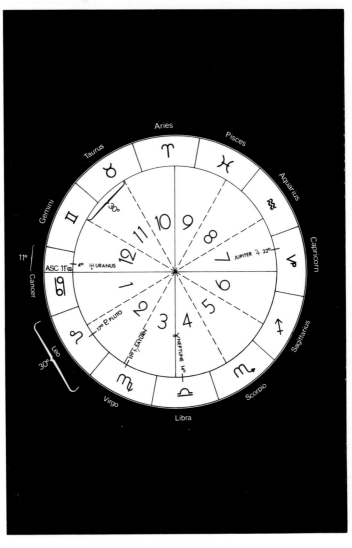

Add the positions of the slow planets – Jupiter, Saturn, Uranus, Neptune, and Pluto.

34

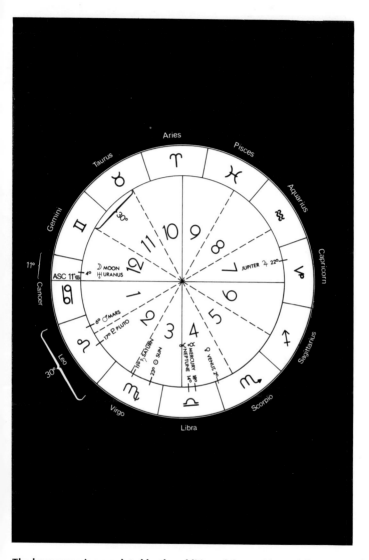

The horoscope is completed by the addition of the positions of the moon, Mars, the sun, Mercury, and Venus.

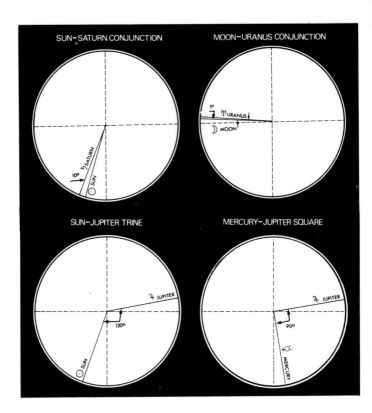

SUN–SATURN CONJUNCTION

SUN–JUPITER TRINE

MOON–URANUS CONJUNCTION

MERCURY–JUPITER SQUARE

Diagrams drawn to illustrate key aspects of the completed horoscope. The conjunction of Sun and Saturn might be worrying, with the gloomy Saturn in the sun-sign and in the third house (of social relationships) – but it is likely that the sun will cancel out the dark planet's effect, because the sun is also trine Jupiter, a very favourable aspect, bringing in the positive outgoing effect of Jupiter. The moon-Uranus conjunction in the twelfth house will underline the streak of powerful emotionalism in the subject, which may trouble her and create difficulties, but also from this conjunction will come an enhanced skill in self-expression, communication and originality. And here again the extraverted side of that sun-Jupiter trine will extend the creative or communicative ability. Mercury square Jupiter is a negative aspect, but not a strong one – perhaps lending Mercury's moody unreliability to the subject's creative, expressive side.

36

as well as degrees – so you can find the 'log' of the birth time (10h 55m) in the same place. It is .3421. You must now add the two log figures: 1.7781 + .3421 = 2.1202.

You next work the thing backwards: you find that figure in the log tables, and its position will give you the degrees and minutes of Mercury's change of position: 0° 11'. And all you do now is go back to the figure you had before, giving the planet's position at noon, and add these two: 18° 2' (of Libra) + 11' = 18° 13'. That's where Mercury was when the subject was born: put it on the horoscope. And then follow the same process for the sun, moon, Mars and Venus.

If the subject had been born in the morning, you would have changed that process in two ways. You would have looked for the planet's position at noon the *day before*. And when you had your final figure for the change of position, you would have *subtracted* it from the figure for noon.

There are also other possible variations, as when planets are 'retrograde' – but the ephemeris kindly tells you how to deal with that, so we may skirt round further complication. The essential thing is that for all practical purposes the horoscope is complete, and contains plenty of information to be extracted.

Reading the Chart

Begin the process by assembling the broad details first, weighing up carefully what they reveal: the nature of the sun-sign and of the ascendant, then the positions of the major planets, all these in terms of the fixed positions of the houses – and certainly any important aspects that might be formed.

It is clearer to demonstrate rather than generalise, so look again at our September-born subject. By sun-sign she is of course a Virgo; note that the Virgo qualities fall into the second and third houses, especially the third where the sun is (the intellectual and self-expressive qualities will be affected by strong Virgo features). But do not forget that Saturn is there too. In fact the sun and Saturn are in the aspect called 'conjunction', in Virgo and the second house, and that can create conflict within the person, since these two planets could not be more different. At the same time, though, conjunction is a strengthening aspect. And a little more use of the protractor on the sun will show that it is 'trine' with Jupiter – enhancing its strength with some of the expansive, extravert, success-oriented qualities of Jupiter. Thus, you might tell the subject that, while Saturn's position is potentially a negative, darkening influence, it can be outweighed by the aspects that strengthen the more positive planets. So there is every chance of success (in occupations to which the Virgo mentality is suited) but it will not be won without some internal struggle, setbacks and periods of gloom.

But we must not neglect the fascinating things that are happening in the ascendant and in the first house – the most personal, the line to the inner self. Cancer is a far different kettle of fish (or crabs) from Virgo, and the presence of these differences will create even more chance of conflict and duality within this person. And Cancerian qualities will be given still further prominence by the presence in it of its own planetary ruler, the changeable and emotional moon.

No question, then, that our subject will suffer strong swings of mood, and tendencies to emotionalism – probably of the darker, depressive sort, for you must note how many of the planets have fallen below the horizon (tending to diminish the importance of the midheaven in this horoscope). At the same time, though, the extra strength of the moon and the sign of Cancer will lend special qualities of imagination, intuition and other *positive* 'emotional' factors to the subject's mind. And here, too, the conjunction with Uranus (a very original, radical planet) will strengthen areas such as originality, independence and communicative ability.

In this way the picture begins to build. Now you must investigate other significant details. Since the two most important signs in this chart are rather 'feminine', how is this view affected by the relative strengths of feminine Venus and masculine Mars? What can be learned from the position of Mercury, ruler of Virgo? Is it at all significant that three planets (including Mercury and loving Venus) fall in the fourth house, area of the formative family and childhood years? Or that fiery, difficult Mars lies in the first house, region of the personal, inner being?

So you may continue for yourself. Make notes as you go, and remember above all three elements that must exist within every single step of your building interpretation. First, *combination*: none of these cosmic events has occurred in isolation, and none must be considered as if it had. The picture must be one of planets-with-planets-in-signs-in-houses, all together, interacting simultaneously.

Second, *balance*: the subject is presumably a functioning person, which means that she has her qualities of character in some sort of equilibrium, without being too seriously undermined by the conflicts and weak points that the chart indicates. So your interpretation must contain balance and equilibrium among the forces, in the same way. This also offsets the possibility of producing an interpretation that could cause distress or anxiety: no fortune teller worthy of the name will throw a gloomy or disturbing prognosis at a subject without stressing the other, positive factors that modify and mitigate it – or perhaps outweigh it altogether,

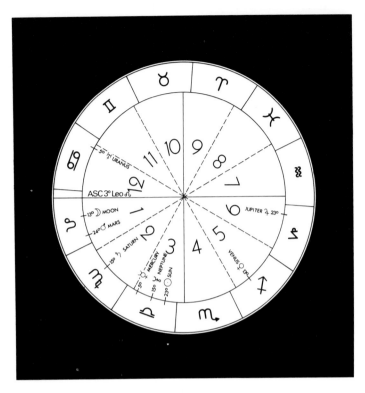

Progressing the sample horoscope to give a reading for 1979 shows the sun in Libra and ascendant in Leo, giving keynotes of balance, adjustment, outer expansion and progress – generally a good prognosis. Moon and Mars nearly in conjunction in the ascendant strengthens Leo's purpose and ambition, with more balance showing ('outward' Mars and 'inward' moon), while moon in Leo is always a good sign for the love life. The theme of balance is stressed again in two important aspects – sun sextile moon and moon sextile Mercury – both of which are beneficial and suggest equilibrium. Jupiter trine Saturn is traditionally a sign of success and advancement in the world – all of which bodes well, with only a few sour notes, as in the sun square Jupiter and some lesser aspects hinting at overwork, overdoing things. The lesson is clear: the subject will have a good year if she maintains the balance and harmony that the horoscope anticipates.

as our sample subject's sun-plus-Jupiter outweigh Saturn.

Third, *flexibility*: never allow your mind to become so fixed on a view of the chart at an early stage that it cannot be adjusted to accommodate later points. Certainly the moon in Cancer in the twelfth house of our subject is of vast importance; but if what we learn from, say, Mars and Jupiter turns out wholly opposed to the Cancerian presence, that data must nonetheless be incorporated, no matter how it may wrench your picture in another direction.

And of course – while the chart that we have composed tells much, and provides an adequate picture – there has been no space for finer details (like special meanings of segments of the signs, or the nodes of the moon and so on). But astrological textbooks exist abundantly where such matters can be pursued (one by Margaret E. Hone is especially well worth having, for those who wish to advance in the art). There, too, you will find further techniques for literally *predicting* the future – rather than, as our chart does, simply spelling out possibilities, potentials and likely directions. One of the most common forms of astrological prediction involves 'progressing' the horoscope – at its simplest, by assuming a connection between a day in the life of the subject after birth and a year in the life overall. So if we were to see what would befall our sample subject in 1979, when she will be thirty, we would cast a horoscope for the thirtieth day after her birth date (i.e. 16 October) – which would reveal much about that year to come. But that would need interpreting no less carefully, with an eye to those three points, than the original birth chart. Just as, in fact, any form of fortune telling – whether cosmic or more intimate, whether personalised or wholly random – needs the same care and the same three-pointed approach as we have learned for the art of the horoscope.

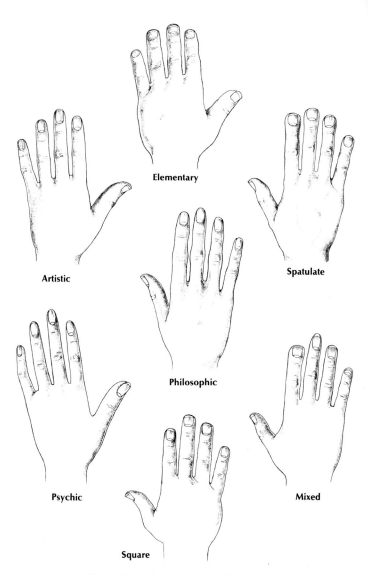

Elementary

Artistic

Spatulate

Philosophic

Psychic

Mixed

Square

The traditional seven types of hand shape

Fortunes
Near at Hand

From reading people's futures in unimaginably distant stars to reading them in their own flesh may seem something of a comedown – but a most natural one. After all, there is a sort of logic in assuming that clues to someone's character and potentialities can be discovered in bumps and wrinkles on his or her body. And that assumption has been, from ancient times till now, the cornerstone of the practice of palmistry.

Palmistry has to do with more than palms, which is why its serious practitioners call it 'chirology' or 'chirognomy' (the Greek *cheir* = hand). Its processes begin – and end – with a consideration of the whole hand. At the outset, this broad, overall picture emerges in the first general hints and impressions about the nature of the hand's owner.

To make this gathering of first impressions simpler and tidier, traditional palmistry suggests specific *types* of hand to look for, always with the proviso that the types, or classifications, are somewhat over-generalised pigeonholes into which few individuals will fit neatly or perfectly. The old-style classification relies a great deal on a rather stereotyped view of social classes – one that will seem medieval at best to people today, progressing as it does through seven stages from the 'brutish' manual labourer to the over-refined aristocrat. Yet the seven types are worth knowing about, if only because elements of that classification have been adapted into less socially biased modern ones.

The traditional seven hand types, then, begin with the 'primitive' or *elementary* hand. Predictably, it is broad, thick, coarse and strong. The heavy palm dominates the hand, with short, thick, stumpy fingers sprouting almost as afterthoughts. Such a hand supposedly reveals a limited, slow mentality and an earth-bound, crude, physical nature – closer to the beast.

Type two is the *square* hand: the palm is square and sturdy, the fingers together are as broad as they are long, even the fingertips are squared off. Here is the hand of practical folk whose horizons are limited – orderly, sensible, conventional, unintellectual and stolid.

The third type is the *spatulate* hand, obviously shaped like a spade or spatula: the palm tapers slightly and the fingertips seem broadened and flattened, again spatula-like. Such people are energetic, restless, often ambitious, certainly independent-minded, though these qualities are more likely to be expressed in non-intellectual sorts of activity.

Type four, though, brings the intellect into the picture. It is the *philosophical* hand, broad of palm and long of finger, often with prominent, knobbly joints. It is the hand of thoughtful, perhaps introverted people – analytical, cautious, pedantic.

The label of the fifth type, the *artistic*, hints at its shape – a long and flexible hand with attractively tapering fingers, the sort of hand an artistic temperament should have. Its owner should have flair and sensitivity, some creative or abstract intellectual ability, a tendency more to impulsiveness, flashes of brilliance and insight, rather than to methodical rationality.

The sixth type takes us even further from people with feet solidly on the ground. It is the *idealistic* hand, also called the 'psychic': long, slender, tapering and aristocratically frail. Its owner will be expected to be delicate, ultra-sensitive, non-physical, impractically dreamy, much given to aesthetics, fantasies and mysticisms.

The seventh type is not really a type at all, but a reminder that the other six types are almost never found in their 'pure' state. It is known as the *mixed* hand; but the mixture can come in a quantity of forms, and the palmist must study hand shapes with care and concentration to pick out the elements of the mixture. One might find a hand with the sturdy palm of the square type but the broad-tipped fingers of the spatulate or the finely tapered fingers of the artistic, and so on. Then it is necessary to work out the relative strengths and importance of these different elements within the overall mixture.

Modern palmists, feeling perhaps that mixtures like these more accurately describe the shapes of hands as they occur in nature, have refined the classification into only four basic types, each of which is 'mixed' to some degree. In this system the first is the *practical* hand, with square palm and short fingers – the hand of hard-working, down-to-earth people whose lives are fairly simple, marked by more physical than mental labour, possibly a bit rough-hewn and narrow-minded but also honest, thrifty and reliable.

The *intuitive* hand has a long palm and short fingers, and reveals an active, nervy, individualistic nature, full of enthusiasms and ambitions, flexible and emotional (a tendency to instability), perhaps creative, often impatient and changeable, sometimes aggressive.

The *sensitive* hand, with a long palm and long fingers, has the delicate and emotional qualities that its label suggests, tending to moodiness, introversion, a passive and secretive approach to life, imaginative (often too much so) and 'feminine' in the traditional, stereotyped sense.

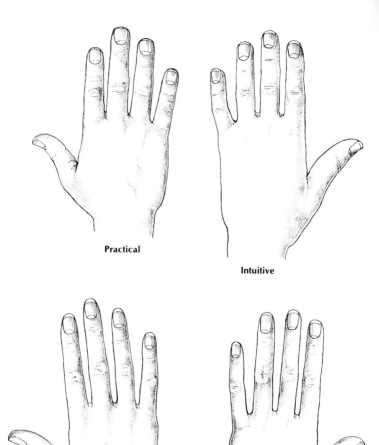

Practical

Intuitive

Sensitive

Intellectual

The modern four types of hand shape

Fourth is the *intellectual* hand, square of palm and long of fingers, revealing high mental capability, quickness of thought and ease of communication – an active, adaptable, rational and orderly nature which can rise to originality or fall victim to dry, over-disciplined, critical tendencies.

Naturally, all these introductory clues plucked from hand types are no more than clues. And often enough the category to which a specific hand belongs will not be entirely apparent until other factors are studied. Other useful hints, though, can still come from first impressions of the whole hand: many palmists make much of skin texture, colour, hairiness and, especially, the *use* of the hands. So it ought to be noted if a subject keeps his or her hands mostly hidden (supposedly showing introversion, insecurity) or makes tight, jerky gestures (tension, aggression) or huge, extravagant gestures (flamboyance, vanity).

But at the same time such indications must be taken with large pinches of salt. They must be viewed as interesting prior indications, and not be allowed to form too hasty or too fixed a view of the person's character. Also, avoid standard stereotyping: not all flabby, damp hands, for instance, reflect flabby, damp personalities. And some of the firmest, manliest handshakes in the world belong to confidence tricksters.

In any case, hand readings these days are often conducted at a distance. The subject sends an ink print (to be looked at again later) of his or her hands, and the palmist studies those, never meeting the person, never seeing gesture, skin texture and the rest. Nor are the readings thus achieved any less complete – because beyond the superficial aspects of the whole hand lie the manifold details, and interrelations, of the parts of the hand. And they provide as much information as anyone could possibly want.

The hand of a woman in her mid-thirties who has been a graphic designer. The general hand-shape tends mostly to the intellectual hand (of the four modern categories), with a squarish palm and fingers proportionately long – but there are elements of the practical hand in the fingers (shapely but not flimsy, with slightly squared tips) and hints of the sensitive hand in the overall palm-shape.

The thumb is long, which suggests liveliness, the (second) phalange of logic hints at some strength of character, but the flexibility of the (upper) phalange of will would make a palmist consider the possibility that the subject might be possessed of too generous, giving, and adaptable a nature. The index finger is a good length, smooth and well shaped, denoting at least the potential of coping well with the outside world and personal ambitions within it; the length of the middle finger intrudes a note of rational control which echoes points made by the intellectual hand-shape and the thumb's second phalange. The ring finger, also in proportion a good length, underlines the element of reason; not being excessively long, it perhaps reflects a well-adjusted emotional being, while its smooth straightness suggests creative ability. The little finger, comparatively short and set slightly apart, may suggest that some of the intuitive, emotional aspects of the personality are similarly 'kept apart' – repressed, or anyway less dominant than the cooler, rational side.

The mount of Venus, below the thumb, not especially prominent but strongly lined, suggests an adequate but not excessive store of life energy, while the prominent bulge of the mount of the moon indicates a good share of inner energy, perhaps not always finding expression. The other, lesser mounts are here not noticeably important: the mount of Jupiter (index finger base) hints slightly at the outer-world involvements, echoing the finger, but not to excess.

The life line is strongly cut and of a good length, which bodes well for the life energies – though badly forked at its beginning, hinting at indecisiveness at an earlier stage. The head line, too, is clean cut and well curved, and lends emphasis to the intellectual and rational side of the subject (note that disruptions, chainings, etc. are minimal). Yet the heart line is set well apart from the head, is chained here and there, and is not particularly long – which a palmist might see as reflecting emotional difficulties, perhaps arising out of the separation of head and heart (and referring back also to the 'apartness' of the little finger). In this context, note that the girdle of Venus is almost non-existent.

With all these elements in mind – though of course with many more lesser indications not touched upon here – the palmist would draw the general impression of a person with 'her head screwed on right', with quite enough energy, talent, and outer-directed life interest to see her through most of the demands, problems and so on that the world may

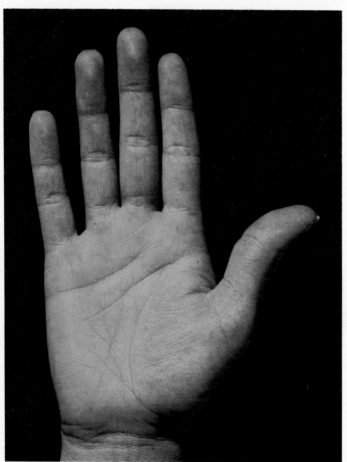

present. But at the same time there are clear hints – less strong, but important – that some areas within the general domain of the emotions have not been wholly catered for, have perhaps been pushed aside or pushed down, have somehow not been brought into full expression or into equilibrium with the 'outer' orientation of the life. However, a palmist would also need to see the other, less-used hand, and to make a more careful study of the minor features of both hands, before reaching any firm conclusion on these matters.

The populous zodiac – Johann Hevelius's depiction of the zodiac signs' personifications and images, from the seventeenth century (British Museum, London).

Astrologers have long found links between the zodiac signs and the body (and diseases), as in this fifteenth-century 'Zodiac man' from the Duke of Berry's 'Très Riches Heures' (Musée Condé, Chantilly).

Fortune telling with the hexagram layout for a fair-haired woman – hence
the queen of hearts as significator. Though the cards in each set round
the circle must be read together, some idea of the interpretation can
be gathered from the top cards shown here. Four of diamonds, in the
'personal matters' position, suggests an unexpected acquisition of
money, probably a legacy or bequest. Three of spades (referring to the
home) is an omen of parting and separation, but it may mean simply
moving house – using that legacy? – because the six of diamonds
(referring to friendship) forecasts harmony and reconciliation. The ten
of spades (referring to the subject's work) foreshadows some worry

52

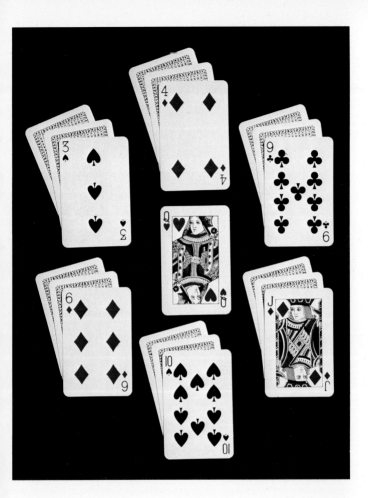

and disturbance, but the knave of diamonds (in the 'inmost feelings' position) may compensate – either by predicting an attractive young man in the subject's life, or some pleasant news. The possibility of a new young man seems to be strengthened by the nine of clubs, in the 'immediate future' position, which is an omen of a romance budding. All in all, the interpretation seems to suggest positive change and pleasant things to look forward to, though not without some moments of unease.

The twenty-two cards of the Tarot's Major Arcana, believed to embody in condensed symbolic form a huge array of occult meaning. 1. The Juggler or Magician (for which the key words would be choice, self-determination). 2. High Priestess (wisdom, hidden knowledge). 3. Empress (fertility). 4. Emperor (power, authority). 5. Pope (spirituality). Next, in this instance, is placed the unnumbered card called the Fool – in essence the card of man as he is, with his contradictions, dualities, strengths and weaknesses. 6. Lovers (love and marriage). 7. Chariot (travel, achievement). 8. Justice – which other Tarot packs might put at number 11 (justice, balance).

9. Hermit (inner wisdom, caution). 10. Wheel of Fortune (good luck). 11. Strength – which might in other packs be number 8 (its key word being its own name, strength). 12. The Hanged Man (pain, growth). 13. Death (its own key word – but also rebirth, renewal). 14. Temperance (moderation, balance). 15. Devil (sexuality, dark tendencies). 16. Falling Tower (misfortune, but hope). 17. Star (positive hope, aid). 18. Moon (dark irrationality). 19. Sun (illumination, good luck). 20. Judgment (achievement, new beginnings). 21. The World (achievement, completion).

The Celtic Cross layout favoured by many Tarot readers. With the Fool as significator, as usual, the first card drawn is placed upon it, and represents the subject's present mental state. The second card, placed across card 1, represents obstacles. Card 3, below the significator, reveals the background; card 4, above, reveals potentialities. Card 5, usually to the left of the significator, reflects the past; card 6, to the right, suggests the future. And four more cards may, optionally, be placed as shown to the right of the whole layout, concerning (top to bottom) the future mental state, future home life, hopes and fears, and finally the answer to some specific question or worry.

Frequently Tarot readers use only the Major Arcana in this layout. But here, we might anticipate a concern with financial affairs in the mental state (card 1, seven of pentacles) perhaps involving some dark opponent (card 2, knight of wands); this may have grown out of a once-stable, balanced state (card 3, two of swords) which is now a state of flux and movement (card 4, eight of wands). But the background contains a measure of strength and authority (card 5, ace of swords), and the future holds signs of a promising, successful outcome (card 6, king of pentacles). The other four cards suggest a future state of mind in which new awareness may emerge out of some difficulty and pain (Hanged Man); some dark young person within the future home life, perhaps not a good influence (knave of swords); some losses but perhaps something inherited (five of cups); and rebirth rather than death as the specific answer (Death).

Chinese sages with the yarrow stalks that originally unlocked the 'oracle' of the 'I Ching' (from a nineteenth-century print).

Omens of the future in random natural sights and happenings: a stork nesting on a chimney (omen of good luck and happiness), a black cat (good luck in Britain, bad in America), a sunny wedding day (good omen for the marriage), the Aurora Borealis (said to be an omen of war), and a comet (a disaster omen, as it was for King Harold in 1066, depicted here on the Bayeux Tapestry).

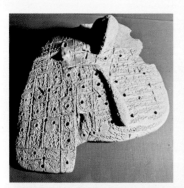

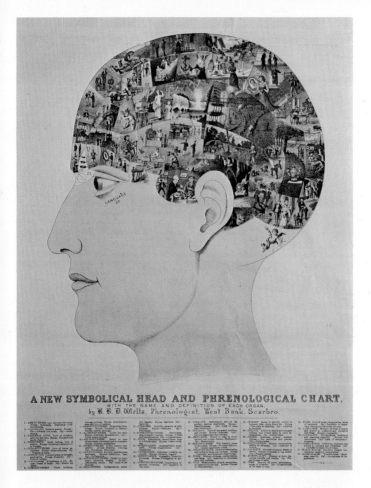

A NEW SYMBOLICAL HEAD AND PHRENOLOGICAL CHART.
WITH THE NAME AND DEFINITION OF EACH ORGAN.
by R. B. D. Wells, Phrenologist, West Bank, Scarbro.

Forms of divination from the ancient world, now mostly obsolete: a
Babylonian clay model of a sheep's liver, marked out to show methods of
entrail reading (British Museum, London); a chart of the areas of the head,
the basis of the art of phrenology; geese in flight, a hopeful omen in
ancient augury; and 'scrying' or gazing for omens in the reflections of a
pool as portrayed by the Pre-Raphaelite painter Edward Burne-Jones in
this detail from 'The Mirror of Venus' (Gulbenkian Foundation, Lisbon).

One of the many versions of the numerological Wheel of Pythagoras –
this one from 1831 (British Library, London).

Painting by Philippe de Champaigne (1602–1674) of the dream-vision of Joseph, instructed by God's messenger to marry Mary (National Gallery, London).

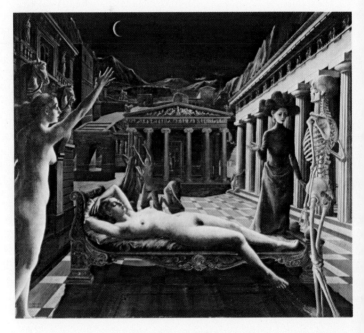

'Venus Asleep', surrealist painting by Paul Delvaux (b. 1879), with the strange, weird, disconnected images that our dreams – and nightmares – usually produce (Tate Gallery, London).

Planetary Fingers

Traditional palmistry refers us back to our first chapter when it comes to the fingers, for each is named after an old deity and therefore connects with the related astrological planet and its qualities. Only the *thumb* has no planetary connection – but palmists link it with the 'first house' of the horoscope, which concerns the subject's self and most personal being.

Palmists also agree that the thumb is by far the most important of the hand's extremities (as it is on a purely physical basis), and they look to it for indication of the owner's share of 'life-force' – the strength, vitality, and potency that is brought to the external existence. The basic rule says that the larger the thumb, the more lively, talented and forceful the nature.

More can be learned from the thumb's separate sections, or 'phalanges'. The nail phalange has to do with the will: a narrow, delicate one suggests energy but indecisiveness and a lack of direction. A broad, sturdy nail phalange means a strong flow of the life-force into clearly seen aims and goals, with plenty of stamina. But a bleak old tradition warns of the abnormally heavy and bulbous ('clubbed') nail phalange, which suggests misdirected or repressed life energies that may sometimes be explosively released without control – which is why this shape was long ago known as the 'murderer's thumb'.

The lower thumb phalange has to do with logic, and if it is full and sturdy it reflects a well-balanced, thoughtful, controlled life – perhaps too controlled and even over-cautious if the phalange is extra-long. A more slender, 'waisted' phalange of logic speaks of much active energy, but it appears in spasmodic bursts, with a risk of headlong impulsiveness.

The joint between the two phalanges should ideally be straight and smooth, indicating the unimpeded flow of life energy into outer concerns. A bumpy, knobby joint indicates, again, the tendency to bursts of energetic activity without much staying power. And those people with especially flexible thumbs which can bend back in a 'double-jointed' way have similarly flexible natures – liberal, adaptable, unconventional but sometimes too generous and too kindly, giving way to more dominating personalities (who will have stiffer thumbs).

The index finger is called the *finger of Jupiter*, and like that lordly planet is related to ambition, dominance, driving

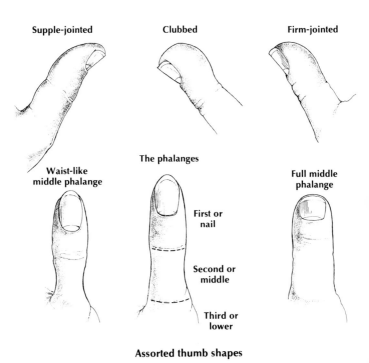

Supple-jointed

Clubbed

Firm-jointed

Waist-like middle phalange

The phalanges

First or nail

Second or middle

Third or lower

Full middle phalange

Assorted thumb shapes

energy. The finger reflects the goals and ambitions, in the outer world, of its owner – so it must be studied in close conjunction with the thumb to see how much life energy there is to be directed towards achieving the goals. A long finger of Jupiter suggests a high level of ambition and drive; but if it is backed up by a weak thumb, there is every chance that the ambition will be frustrated, leading to bitterness, envy and psychological stress.

A shortish index finger may merely mean a lack of staying power, but a disproportionately short one suggests a definite lack of confidence. A thick finger of Jupiter means dogged determination, a slender one means that the ambitions are more hopes and dreams than active, driving intentions. Smooth joints indicate a streak of emotive or intuitive strength within the life processes, while knotted joints signify a more analytical, logical approach.

The second or middle finger is named after gloomy, chilly old *Saturn*, so it is no wonder that palmists look for comparable sombreness in the finger. Its shape serves as indicator of mental balance or imbalance: if it is unusually long, there is a threat of the latter. (And if the nail phalange alone is unduly long, there is a suggestion of outright mental illness with suicidal tendencies – though, happily, that finger shape is a rare phenomenon.) But the imbalance of a finger slightly longer than ordinary may take the form merely of a social coolness, a dry and withdrawn ('saturnine') personality for whom forming relationships is neither easy nor particularly desirable. A shorter middle finger suggests a strong intuitive and perhaps creative element – which might overbalance into the other extreme, with an abnormally short finger, into hypersensitive and possibly hysterical tendencies.

The progress across the fingers from the thumb side is a movement from outer to inner matters, from rational to emotional, conscious to unconscious. So the middle finger, of Saturn, stands on the dividing line, which is why it is linked with questions of balance. The ring finger, called the *finger of Apollo*, takes on some of the astrological qualities of the sun: it is the finger of the emotions, which can enhance life as can a warm, benevolent sun or can cripple and warp life as can, at other times, the sun's blistering heat. It is also the finger most indicative of creative ability (Apollo was the god of art and invention as well as a sun god).

A short ring finger denotes a lack of emotional control, a likelihood of high emotionalism undermining the chance of an easy progress through life. A longer finger of Apollo shows the opposite: not emotional outbursts but emotional withdrawal, introversion, perhaps feelings of inferiority. A smooth finger with smooth joints suggests pronounced and potentially successful creative abilities. If the ring finger does not stand straight (when the hand is held open and relaxed), but bends and droops towards the palm, then its owner has problems coming to terms with the intuitive, unconscious aspects of the personality.

The little finger is the *finger of Mercury*, and brings in the realm of human relationships, especially those more emotionally based. A long little finger shows high intelligence and orientation to learning and to skill at self-expression, the more so if the extra length comes mainly in the first phalange. A short finger of Mercury traditionally hints at some mental deficiency, a twisted one supposedly reveals dishonesty. And the placement of this finger is crucial: if it is set widely apart from the other fingers, it suggests some difficulty with human (above all, sexual) relationships – all the more difficulty if it also bends, when at rest, down towards the palm.

But palmistry places similar importance on the relative

positions of *all* the fingers. A thumb set rather low on the hand indicates a repression of the life energies. An index finger bent in towards the others reveals some degree of acquisitiveness – with a slight bend, perhaps the mild form of a hobbyist's 'collecting', but with a pronounced bend, the obsession of a hoarder or miser. And a middle finger that bends one way or the other shows whether the owner inclines more to the rational or irrational aspects of life.

If the ring finger bends (especially its nail phalange) towards the middle finger, again there is emotional mal-adjustment. And older texts, following the mistaken medieval notion that a special artery ran straight to the heart

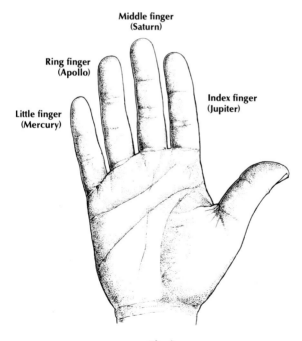

Middle finger (Saturn)

Ring finger (Apollo)

Index finger (Jupiter)

Little finger (Mercury)

The fingers

from this finger, still suggest that a bend of the ring finger forewarns of heart ailments. But that old wives' tale is today viewed only metaphorically – that a bent ring finger warns of 'afflictions of the heart' in the emotional, love-relationship sense.

Up on the Mounts

Just as the lengths, shapes and settings of the fingers must be read in relation to one another, for the overall picture the fingers must also be studied in relation to the fleshy regions of the palm which are called the *mounts*. So no full understanding can be gained of, first, the all-important thumb without a close look at the area from which it rises – the *mount of Venus*.

This mount reflects the life energies as much as the thumb: it is often called the 'storehouse' of those energies, in all their forms. A well-developed mount of Venus shows abundant physical energy, not to mention a high sexuality, as might be expected from its association with the goddess of love. If the lower part of the mount is especially prominent, it suggests the sort of energy that can be channelled into artistic activity, all the more so if the mount is scored by a great many lines.

Across the hand is another area of equal importance, the *mount of the moon*. Since the moon is linked with irrational matters, in astrology and other traditions, this mount refers to such matters as well – imagination, intuition, creativity, the unconscious mind. So while the 'practical' type of hand ought to have a large mount of Venus, for the physical activity element, it is the 'sensitive' hand where a sizeable mount of the moon will likely occur. In a nutshell, the mount of Venus reflects life-forces directed outwards, the mount of the moon indicates those directed inwards. Extensive lines and whorls on the moon mount can mean too much inward-ness — an overdeveloped imagination, dreaminess. And a weak mount of the moon can mean changeableness to the point of outright instability.

The lesser mounts occur at the bases of the fingers and take their names and some of their associations from them. A prominent *mount of Jupiter* will reinforce the finger's suggestion of driving ambition: be ready to adjust your view of the subject's outer ambitions if both mount and finger are strong, if both are weak, or if one is strong and the other contradictorily weak. The *mount of Saturn* underwrites its finger's link with personality balance: if large, the mount

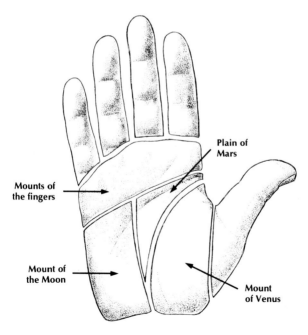

Plain of Mars

Mounts of the fingers

Mount of the Moon

Mount of Venus

The principal mounts of the hand

emphasises the element of high seriousness, which might be morose depressive tendencies if the mount is extra-large. A sizeable *mount of Apollo* means an extra share of an outgoing nature, charming and generous. A prominent *mount of Mercury* can mean that, within what the little finger shows about the owner's closer relationships, there is a tendency to be standoffish and critical. This mount, if strong, is also said to indicate shrewd business ability. Just below it some palmists pick out an even smaller mount, of *Mars*, which shows one's ability to stand up for oneself; but not many hands exhibit this mount as a visibly separate prominence.

Along the Lines

Now, at last, head full of information, the palmist comes to gather the crucial data available in those criss-cross creases that are the *lines* of the palm. Because their interactions are so important, there is no required order in which to approach them. The *life line* seems as good a starting place as any.

Traditional palmists, and their none-too-careful modern equivalents of funfair and back-street, have presented the life line as simply the measurement of life span. And in so doing they have no doubt thrown many clients with short life lines into icy panic. But modern experts insist that it simply is not so. The life line represents much the same thing as the thumb and mount of Venus (it is the demarcation line of the latter): life-force and energies, the presence or absence of vitality. The longer the line and the deeper it is cut, the more abundant are the life energies – including physical robustness, stamina, drive and so on. But a short line does not necessarily denote a weakling or invalid. It can serve merely as a warning that the energy store is limited, and so must be husbanded, expended wisely and sparingly.

Watch also for the particular quality of the line (the

illustrations will clarify these points). A *broken* life line suggests some disruption, upheaval, change of direction in the subject's life – and the extent of the break shows how serious this alteration is, or will be. Sometimes such disruptions may be to do with a physical upheaval (illness, say, quelling the life energy) but as often the changes happen in the outer life circumstances. A *chained* life line suggests that the energies are not consistent, but manifest themselves in short, uneven bursts. A *wavy* life line means a 'wavy', unsure, vacillating character. An *island* on the line foreshadows a period of physical weakness or susceptibility, though not as serious a disruption as a pronounced break.

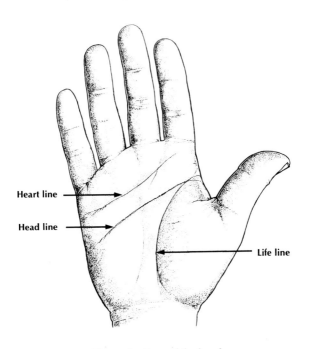

Heart line

Head line

Life line

The major lines of the hand

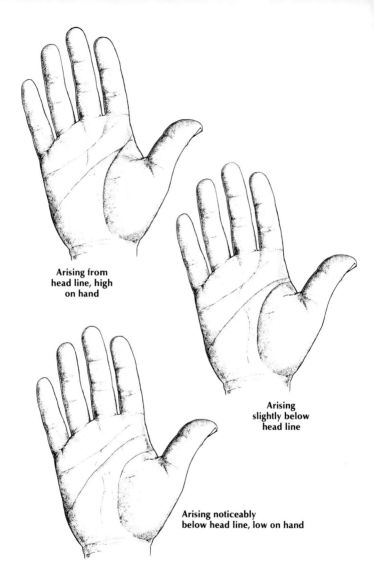

Arising from head line, high on hand

Arising slightly below head line

Arising noticeably below head line, low on hand

Three starting places of the life line

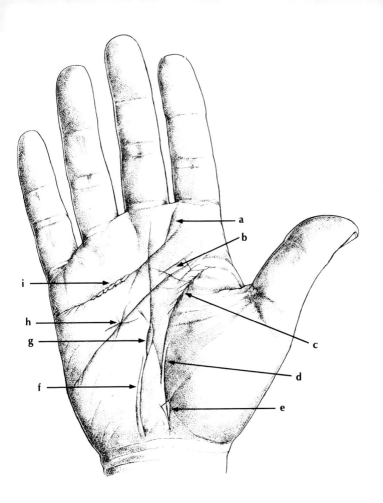

Markings on the lines

a Fork on heart line
b Square on head line
c Branching on life line
d Partial (overlapping) break on life line
e 'Triangle' on life line
f Doubling of fate line
g 'Island' on fate line
h 'Star' on head line
i 'Chaining' on heart line

If the life line starts high on the hand (its terminal 'end' is down towards the wrist), it will enhance some of the attributes of the finger of Jupiter, the ambition, determination and so on. If the line begins well below the head line, it indicates a lack of control and of inhibition – the head, in short, not mastering or directing the energies. If the life line arises actually from the head line, then the head – the reason – is fully in charge, and the person will be cool, logical, controlled, perhaps to the extreme of being extra-clever or coldly calculating.

Never forget to assess the life line against the background of the thumb and mount of Venus, to see whether what you have learned from those features is confirmed, extended, qualified or contradicted. In the same way the *head line* – stretching from the mount of Jupiter across to the mount of the moon – must be read in conjunction with those features.

The head line obviously concerns the 'head' sort of factors: mentality, intellect, reason and logic, discipline and the rest. A short and none-too-distinct line shows that intellectual matters do not feature prominently in the person's life. It does *not* show the depth or extent of native intelligence, but only what use is made of the intellectual potential. So the longer the line, the wider the scope of intellectual activity. And the more clear and distinct it is, the stronger are the subject's powers of concentration and self-discipline. A chained head line shows a scatty tendency to concentrate in fits and starts, while a doubled head line, like a railway track, shows almost no ability to concentrate at all.

The curve of the head line also reveals much. It should sweep smoothly in a slight curve down towards the mount of the moon, which introduces a leavening of imagination and intuition into the rational mental processes. Too pronounced

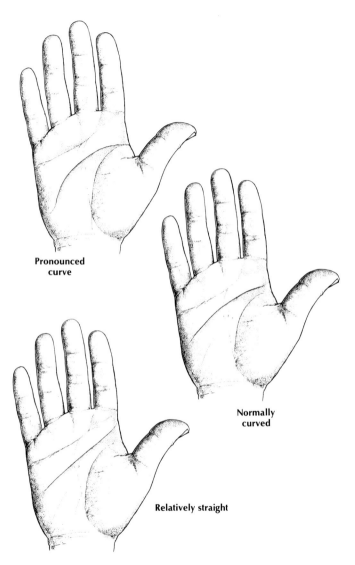

Pronounced curve

Normally curved

Relatively straight

Three types of curve on the head line

a downward curve and the intellect is marred by a fanciful tendency. Too straight a line, and the intellect is limited by an over-logical lack of imagination.

Any clear breaks on the line indicate as always change and disruptions. A major break can pinpoint a major mental disturbance — not necessarily mental illness, perhaps some shattering event that leaves its mark on the mind. Slighter disruptions may coincide instead with less disturbing changes of direction, like new interests, new avenues of intellectual activity. And a fork also indicates some side-routing of the mental interest or activity, either indecision or the simultaneous pursuit of two separate avenues.

Above the head line, the equally well-named *heart line* portrays the nature of the subject's emotional inner being, including the sexuality. So, again, a long and clear line indicates emotional depth and balance and a healthy attitude to sex. It is interesting that some palmists say they seldom encounter such lines these days . . .

If the heart line begins high on the hand, the emotionalism and sexuality are correspondingly stronger; conversely, a heart line that runs down close to the head line implies some limitation from the rational, 'head' side — a lack of passion, indifferent to (or inhibited about) matters of love and sex.

Chainings and breaks occur more often on the heart line than on the others, and predictably indicate emotional difficulties, upheavals, 'heartbreak' and so on. Excessive chaining suggests emotional inconsistency and perhaps also fickleness in love. Breaks on the line need not be signs of disruptions in the love life, but may indicate other sorts of emotional dislocations.

The heart line also provides one of the clear points where science, to the delight of palmists, has confirmed the old traditions. One rare variation of the line occurs when the

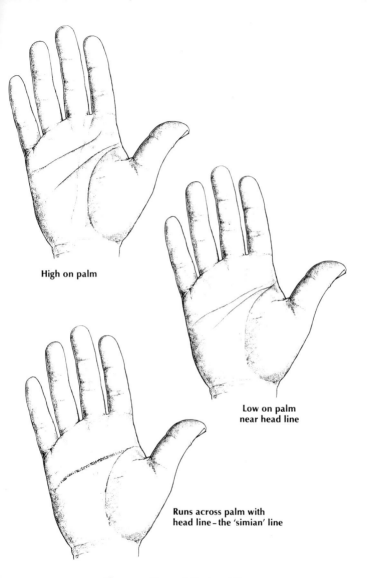

High on palm

Low on palm
near head line

Runs across palm with
head line – the 'simian' line

Three positions of the heart line

79

heart and head lines run together, or nearly so, as one line – probably a badly cluttered and disrupted one. This marking is usually now called the *simian line*, because it occurs almost invariably in the higher apes. Palmists of the past saw it as a special sort of 'bestial' marking, and took it as a sign of 'degeneracy', criminality, mental disorder or mental defectiveness, all rather cruelly lumped together. Medical researchers today, as it happens, have found that the simian line does occur fairly often among habitual criminals with low-order mentalities – but that it occurs with much more reliable regularity in certain cases of mental retardation. In fact many doctors, especially in America, will today look for such a line in the palms of newborn babies – as an early-warning sign of mongolism, or of the sorts of defects that can occur when the mother has had German measles during pregnancy.

Still, the average palmist may go through an entire career and never meet such a blurring of the head and heart lines. He or she will meet the more common lesser lines of the palm, however, and of these the 'line of destiny' takes precedence.

Also called the *fate line*, this marking varies most widely from one hand to another. It should begin near the wrist and run vertically towards the finger of Saturn, neatly dividing the hand in two (in fact separating the outer/inner, mental/emotional dualities). The stronger and longer the line, the more favourable is the prognosis for the subject's future. Apparently the line reveals strength and equilibrium of personality, ability to adapt to changing circumstances, to overcome obstacles, to win through to goals. So the more indistinct or disrupted or shaky lines reflect personalities that could be similarly described – not good omens for balanced and fulfilled lives. But at the same time this line shows a considerable tendency to alter (as all lines can and do, to some extent) over the years, so the judgment of the destiny taken from one reading of the fate line is by no means absolute.

Next is the *girdle of Venus,* to be read especially in conjunction with the heart line, for it reveals the extent – or lack – of the subject's sensuality and passions. One would not expect a strong girdle of Venus on a hand that otherwise shows a practical, controlled, rational person (but one might be surprised).

The *line of Apollo* is a small line running from near the

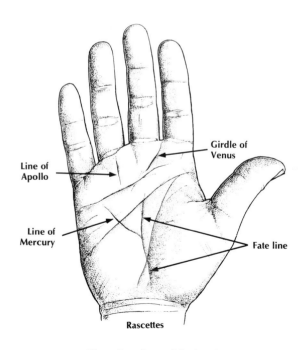

Girdle of Venus

Line of Apollo

Line of Mercury

Fate line

Rascettes

The minor lines of the hand

heart line towards the finger of Apollo, and may show creative ability or at least the sort of emotional range and depth usually associated with creativity. And even more minor is the *line of Mercury*, angling away from the fate line towards the mount of Mercury – not always visible in many hands, but said to indicate some degree of extrasensory or 'psychic' ability. It would be a useful line for a would-be fortune teller to find in his or her own hand; but many get along very well without it.

Finally there are the lines round the wrist called the 'bracelets' or *rascettes*. Three of them, well delineated, form a good sign of health and wealth and fulfilled ambition. If the upper one is strongly arched (towards the palm) in a woman, she may have difficult childbirth. If the bracelets are chained or indistinct, obstacles will confront the owner, and much work and struggle will be needed to achieve their desires in life.

Reading Between the Lines

The sub-heading above is not intended to be merely jocular. There is more to interpreting all the elements of a hand than reciting the straightforward 'meanings' outlined in this chapter. A good interpretation will be more than the sum of its parts. And so the interpreter needs to bring an open and flexible mind to the job – and to *maintain* that openness of mind until every jot of data is gathered. Nothing can destroy interpretation more quickly than forming a theory, too soon and too rigidly, about the subject's personality and prospects – for people tend to twist later data to fit their preformed theory. Form early impressions, yes; but be always ready to adjust them, adapt them, even abandon them if necessary as the reading goes on.

To be done properly, interpretation must be taken slowly

and with the utmost concentration. You cannot sit down with your subject and reel off a useful interpretation straight away. Much better, if palmistry is to be taken seriously (and if not, it is best left alone), to take some sort of an image of the hands in question, to be studied and pored over at leisure.

A palmist with a Polaroid camera can take photographs of the hands — more than one, from different angles and lightings, to show up all the markings. But most palmists prefer to take *prints*, which perfectly reveal lines, mounts, finger lengths and everything that is necessary. The process is simple, and not as messy as it may sound.

You use the basic kit that is used for making 'linocuts', for it provides the water-based (easily removable) ink and small roller. You also need some sort of highly smooth surface (a sheet of stainless steel or glass) and some good quality white paper. Squeeze ink on to the glass or metal and roll it out to spread a film of ink smoothly on the roller; then roll ink on to the subject's hand, equally smoothly, from wrist to finger-tip. Then carefully place the hand on to the sheet of paper — under which there should be other sheets of paper and perhaps a rubber mat (of the sort that goes under a type-writer). Press the hand down slightly, to ensure a firm print, but be careful not to let the hand slip or slide or to let the paper move.

A very little practice will improve your print-making skills, and will be worth it. You will have the chance to study the hand at length, and you will also have a record — for a kind of cumulative comparison — of hands you have read. Perhaps more practice will be needed to improve your inter-pretative skills, for experience means much in this area.

Most of the tips for interpretation have already been scattered through this chapter, most of all the need to build

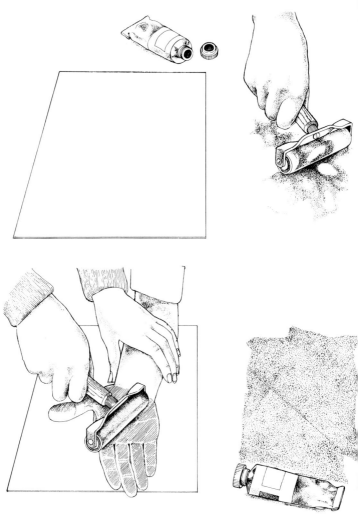

Four easy steps in taking a print of a palm, for reading. One: squeeze out ink on smooth surface, then roll it out to spread ink over roller. Two: thoroughly ink all surfaces of palm, fingers, thumb and mounts, using roller to give a smooth and even distribution of ink. Three: place hand

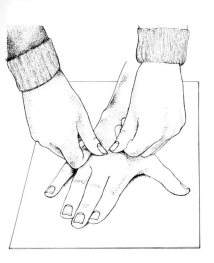

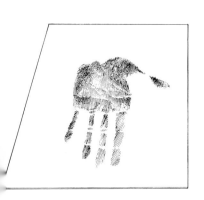

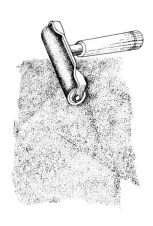

carefully onto prepared pad of paper (with rubber pad beneath) so that hand lies with its natural, usual placing of fingers; press down gently to ensure a full print of every feature. Four: lift hand away carefully, ensuring that neither the hand nor the paper slips to blur the print.

an overall picture, especially regarding those parts of the hand that pertain to the same sort of factors. Does, for instance, the heart line add to the impression that you got from the little finger, or belie it? Does the quality of the life line reflect what is indicated by the shape of the whole hand, the middle finger, the thumb – or does it diverge from these elements? When questions like these are being asked and answered, a worthwhile (flexible and thoughtful) interpretation is building.

With flexibility, though, use caution as well. Very few individual hands are glaringly one thing or another. There may seem to be elements of all four basic hand types present: you must carefully, patiently sort out which are predominant. All the fingers and thumb may wildly contradict and undermine one another: you must cautiously work out the most significant, operative features of each – and so on.

One other tip might be helpful. Palmists say that the hand which a person uses least (the left hand of a right-handed person) shows in all its markings the *potentials* with which that person was born. And the hand he or she uses most shows what has been made of those potentials, so far. Useful clues can be gained, then, from comparing elements in one hand and then the other. A heart line set well away from the head line in the 'potentials' hand, suggesting over-emotionalism, may have been brought down in the other hand, showing that the head has controlled and curbed this tendency. A chained head line in one hand may be a clear, sharp line in the other. A broken fate line in one may be mended in the other.

You may want to seek aid, in your early stages, from other books by recognised authorities; but take care here, too. Stay away from older texts, for more modern writers will have incorporated whatever is useful from the older tradition but will also, valuably, have sieved away much of the dross of superstition and folklore. And read any authority with a pinch of salt, taking nothing as absolute and fixed gospel for all cases. Use them as guides only – but do use them, for as you progress you will want to know more about the lesser lines, minor markings and all the relationships, more than this chapter could hope to include.

And use caution in one more thing: what you tell your subjects. To put it bluntly, there is no telling how suggestible people are – even those who like to scoff disbelievingly at all this 'mumbo-jumbo'. Even if you see a clear sign in a hand of major disruption, disaster, disease, take care. You could be over-emphasising some element; you could be over-looking some modifying influence; you could simply be mistaken. So moderate your interpretation, for seeds of anxiety are planted easily and sprout readily in people, but are confoundedly difficult to uproot.

Finally, a point that applies to every suggestion made so far, and to every form of fortune telling: do not be afraid to listen to your instincts, your subjective emotional responses, your intuitions. Reading palms is not a remote, intellectual exercise any more than it is a game. Do not merely plod step by ritual step through the parts of the hand: if by some intuitive 'flash' you spot a cross-connection from one element to another, or if several separate items seem to slide together into a pattern, take hold of that 'flash', note it down, do not forget it. That is the level on which the great fortune tellers make their most remarkable perceptions. The functioning of the intuition cannot of course be summoned; but it ought never to be ignored. And certainly the intuitive, emotional responses ought to play an especially vital role when the material being studied by the fortune teller is the living flesh of another human being's hand.

The Wheel of Fortune card-reading layout: in a circle round the significator, eight sets of three cards each are dealt (see page 101 for directions) and a ninth set below. Cards are numbered in order of deal.

Dealing Out Destiny

Astrology and palmistry, both of course bedrock to the art of fortune telling, also both tend more towards the 'character-reading' side – working out what kind of person the subject is, the elements of the psychological nature, and only from that going on to formulate the potentials and prospects. With the long-lived art of *cartomancy*, however, the fortune teller enters a more magical and overtly 'occult' world, in which the techniques of the reading come together to spell out, directly and immediately, details about the future.

At the same time, reading futures in ordinary playing cards offers the newcomer another beautifully simple means of taking up the art and craft of divining. Few homes these days are without a pack of cards, and you need nothing more. Each card has its fixed, traditional meaning and set of associations; and once these have been grasped and remembered, there is very little more to it, other than knowing some of the patterns in which the cards can be dealt out for a reading. There is no reason why anyone with this chapter at hand could not begin a tentative reading within a few minutes of completing this sentence.

Many fortune tellers like to introduce an element of magicality at the outset of a reading, if only to build up the atmosphere. Generally the idea is to bring the subject into things, supposedly to 'tune in' the cards to the subject's individuality. So the fortune teller may begin by thoroughly shuffling the cards and then inviting the subject to cut them; or the subject may be asked to do all the shuffling and cutting. Cards are usually cut three times, with the left hand and towards the left (symbolically the side of magic and the supernatural). While all this is going on the subject is to concentrate on matters of special concern – ambitions, hopes, anxieties – or on particular questions that the reading might illuminate.

The reader then takes over, and first seeks the card that will represent the subject – which card is called the *significator*. A good few rituals exist for selecting the right card, but most readers simply search through the pack for what tradition says is the proper significator. The tradition is both obvious and simplistic, for it makes connections between the court cards and the sex, marital status and appearance of the subject.

If the subject is a 'fair' (i.e. fair-skinned and light-haired) man, his significator must be the king of hearts.

If a dark man, his significator is the king of clubs.

If a fair (blonde) woman, the queen of hearts. It can also be used for any young, unmarried woman.

If a red-haired or light-brown-haired woman, the queen of diamonds. Also used for any young, married woman.

If a dark-brown-haired or black-haired woman, the queen of clubs. Often used only for married brunettes; also for any more mature married woman.

Once a significator has been chosen, the court card of the opposite sex in that suit will represent (should it turn up in the reading) the spouse, or beloved, of the subject. So if you are reading cards for a dark married woman, her significator is the queen of clubs and the king of clubs would be her husband.

If the subject is a widow, her significator is the queen of

The hearts suit of modern cards descends from the Tarot's chalices suit, and connects with love and pleasure; diamonds (Tarot pentacles) with money; clubs (wands) with work; spades (swords) with ill luck.

spades – and the king of spades for a widower. Up-to-date readers sometimes use these also for divorced folk, but others prefer to treat such subjects as single.

Knaves (jacks) were once used for young men, but today most readers prefer to see knaves (should they turn up) as representing other male influences on the subject. Sometimes, for male subjects, the knaves can be taken not as other people but as reflections of the subject's own inner thoughts and tendencies.

Clearly you will be allowed some latitude, then, in selecting a significator. And you may be guided further by the traditional and very important associations that are attached to each suit in general. *Hearts*, first, are the cards of love, friendship and pleasure. *Diamonds* have to do with money matters (the older European name for diamonds was Coins). *Clubs* are associated with work, and with related virtues like reliability, honour, thrift and the like. *Spades*, the gloomy suit, have to do with ill luck, violence (their old name was Swords) and disasters in general.

So a clever reader might choose the king or queen of diamonds as significator for a rich subject, whatever the hair colour; or the king of spades for a military man, whatever his hair colour or marital status.

Meanings at Court

From these overall associations with the suits come some of the more specific meanings of each individual card. It must be said straight away that the meaning of any one card in a reading may be affected by adjacent cards. But a knowledge of their separate meanings is essential, especially the court cards. They tend to represent individuals who will enter or influence the subject's life – as opposed to the forces or tendencies represented by the numbered cards.

King of hearts. An important man of fair complexion, possibly of high rank or distinction; good-natured, affectionate and generous.

Queen of hearts. All the traditional virtues embodied in the male chauvinist's ideal wife: attractive (and fair-complexioned), loving and lovable; strong, generous, even-tempered; above all faithful and devoted.

Knave of hearts. May be taken as standing for a male subject's best male friend. Otherwise it refers to a young man, usually a bachelor, fair, charming and pleasure-loving; but sometimes a bit of a rascal and an impostor (remember who it was in the nursery rhyme who stole the tarts).

King of diamonds. Usually a well-off businessman or someone very involved with money-making; perhaps an older man, grey-haired; strong, thrifty, determined, but possibly also ambitious and thrusting to the point of ruthlessness.

Queen of diamonds. An attractive, chic woman of the world, flirtatious and sexy, perhaps tending to go too far in pursuit of fashion, pleasure and extravagance; also something of a gossip.

Knave of diamonds. A pleasant and talented young man, also ambitious, often to the point of single-minded self-interest; potentially successful but not all that known for reliability or loyalty; possibly also a messenger of some sort.

King of clubs. A dark man who represents the female chauvinist's traditional view of the ideal husband – strong, loyal, reliable, sensible, kind, intelligent and loving (not necessarily in that order).

Queen of clubs. An attractive dark woman, both sexy and affectionate, intelligent with a good sense of humour, but with a chance of a moody, unpredictable temperament and perhaps too sexually oriented.

Knave of clubs. A dark young man, and/or a true and honest friend; intelligent, with initiative and integrity; perhaps with a tendency to be either somewhat too sensitive or too extravagant.

King of spades. An aggressive, dominating, probably successful man, dangerous if an enemy; perhaps a military man, usually a dark, mature man.

Queen of spades. Often a widow, as mentioned; otherwise a darkly attractive woman who can be a treacherous *femme fatale*, using her wiles to gain wealth or power.

Knave of spades. An equally dark and dangerous young man, attractive but selfish, a seducer and betrayer, sometimes an outright criminal.

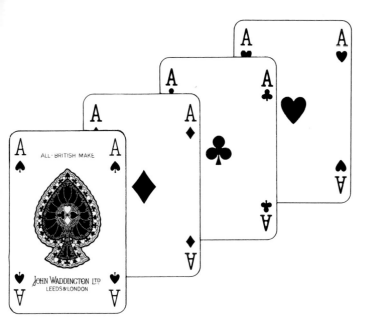

Meanings of Aces

Ace of hearts. Affairs of the heart and also the home – a romance blossoming or happy domestic activities and rewarding friendship; also a sign of good news on the way.

Ace of diamonds. The arrival of money and/or important letters; sometimes also a betrothal or a marriage.

Ace of clubs. A card of good fortune, often in terms of finance, also welcome letters or other news.

Ace of spades. Sometimes a dire card, heralding bad news and worse luck, misfortune of various kinds; but some card readers see in it a sign merely of forthcoming legal matters, not necessarily unfortunate.

The lesser cards receive less interpretive scope. Leading with hearts, again: the two foretells a friend; the three, pleasure; four, a change; five, money coming; six, unexpected luck; seven, good news; eight, a lover or visitor; nine, success; ten, happiness.

In diamonds: two, a warning; three, socialising; four, a legacy; five, an encounter; six, reconciliation; seven, a child or a gift; eight, money or a journey; nine, news, or some new venture; ten, a journey, or unexpected income.

Clubs: two, a novelty; three, friends; four, pleasure; five, an enemy; six, encouragement; seven, money coming; eight, a dark lover; nine, inheritance; ten, prosperity, travel.

Spades: two, treachery; three, a loss or separation; four, calm; five, sadness; six, change or upheaval; seven, difficulties; eight, sorrow, illness; nine, grief, loss (some say death); ten, worry, a journey.

Connecting the Cards

The aces can provide useful examples of the sort of modification and cross-connection that occurs when cards come together to be read. Because the ace of hearts has to do with the home, when it turns up among other hearts it will underline the love relationships centred on the home. If it appears among many diamonds, it suggests money on the way into the home. If surrounded by clubs, it will suggest general good luck on the home front; if by spades, some bad luck at home.

And so on through the aces, making the straightforward connections between the 'areas of operation' of each ace and each suit. Also, if the aces fall naturally together, there may be a considerable change in the subject's life – a change of job, of direction, of dwelling, etc. (Other factors in the reading will show whether this change will be beneficial or disastrous.)

The kings coming together, even three of them, foretell reward or achievement – business profits, promotion, honours or the like. The queens together warn of gossip and scandal, though only three can mean merely a pleasant visitor. The knaves together predict some major row or other disturbance, a less serious one if only three.

A few similar groupings 'of a kind' are extended to lower value cards. Four tens mean financial benefit (not so large if only three or two tens). Eights reflect family matters: four can mean trouble on that front, three or two mean merely some changes. Four sevens may warn of treachery by friends; less than four, only minor troubles and setbacks.

Such meaningful combinations could be extended for thousands more words, but space allows only a limited further sampling. The two red aces together foretell an enjoyable invitation; the two black ones, sudden news from afar. Aces of diamonds and spades together: a journey. Two black nines mean bad news, two red nines good news. Ace of diamonds with ten of hearts, a betrothal. Queen of spades and ten of spades, danger. Any queen with any knave, a possible secret affair. Ace of diamonds and nine of spades, a danger of ill health. Ace and nine of spades, a serious disappointment. Eight of diamonds and any club, another journey.

And if your friendly gypsy fortune teller turns pale and brings your reading to an abrupt end, she may have turned up the most awesomely frightful portent of all – the combination of ace, nine, seven and four of spades, which means total calamity and even death.

But even then there is no point in becoming too morbid, and certainly no point in implanting terror and anxiety into someone for whom you have turned these cards up. As ever in fortune telling, you must look to the 'big picture', the overall shape and direction of the reading. When all the elements have been weighed into the interpretation, even that most fearsome of portents might be seen to be diminished in importance or counteracted.

Laying Out the Cards

Before interpreting, however, you must have something to interpret. And though there are a few simple tricks for instant, one-off hints, right down to the 'take a card, any card' level, readers usually prefer to achieve more detail by using one of the standard *layouts* for fortune telling.

To begin with, a simple layout – made even simpler because it uses only thirty-two cards, removing all the lower cards from twos to sixes. After the usual shuffle, the cards are cut (right to left, and always face down) into three more or less equal piles. These represent, from the left, the subject's past, present and future. The reader then takes each stack in turn, spreading out the cards, noting whether any one suit predominates, what combinations occur, finally commenting on each individual card.

It is also useful not to remove a significator for the subject but to see if it turns up in one of the three stacks, suggesting which aspect or time of his or her life is most important. As a variation, some readers take two cards off the top of the thirty-two, after the shuffle (they can then deal, rather than cut, into three equal stacks). These two are kept aside, face down, till the reading is over, and then produced to signify some wholly unexpected event or effect that is approaching.

Another popular layout is called the *hexagon* or *hexagram* (see page 53). Remove the significator and place it face up on the table. Shuffle as always, then deal six cards (face down, moving round to the left) in a circle around the significator. Then go round twice more so that the circle is finally composed of six stacks with three cards in each. (The rest of the pack is put aside.) The first stack dealt represents personal matters affecting the subject. The second refers to the home; the third to a close friend; the fourth to the job or career; the fifth to something 'close to the subject's heart'; the sixth to the immediate future. Within these six frameworks the separate stacks are turned up and their omens interpreted.

Variations of this circular layout can be found in a layout where the deal creates eight stacks, each with three cards, each roughly at one point of an eight-pointed star (page 102). Similarly there is the *Wheel of Fortune* (page 88), where each pile again holds three cards, though the sets of three are dealt out three at a time, rather than going round the circle dealing out one card at a time, at each position.

A little traditional chant goes with the deal in this layout: 'three above you, three below you, three behind you, three before you, three for your hearth and home, three for your hopes and fears, three for the unexpected, three for the expected, three for the certain future.' Which means that the cards in each stack refer to, in order, influences or controls on ('above') the subject; matters under ('below') the subject's influence or control; the past ('behind'); the immediate future; domestic matters; and the rest are self-explanatory.

More layouts than most of us will ever have time to try could be found in the shelves-full of books about card-reading. And dipping into some of these – especially the more modern and less pretentious ones – might offer some ideas. But the few layouts already mentioned here will suffice for the time needed to become familiar with the

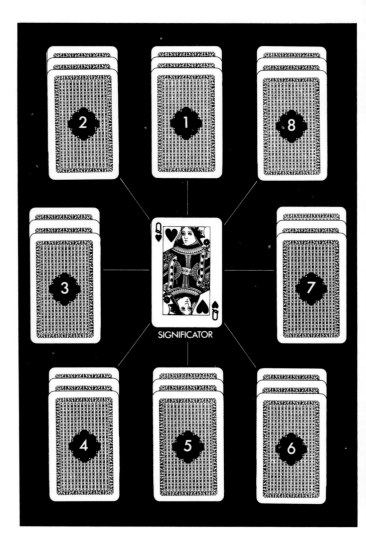

The eight-pointed star layout ends with eight sets of three cards each in a circle round the significator. The first set is dealt above the centre, the others in order counterclockwise.

meanings of the cards and their combinations – and should suffice also to provide the experience needed to feel at home with the art of interpreting the cards.

By now it should not be necessary to include the reminder that interpretation is more than just reeling off memorised meanings. Again, you must let your intuition – about the subject of the reading, about the images that build and form with the cards' fall – have free rein. Try to know something about the subject beforehand: the basic 'age, sex and occupation' that you should always know for any form of fortune telling, but also some hints and early impressions of the personality and potentials. Then you can more easily be guided through complexity: you will decide more readily whether, say, a multitude of hearts implies much activity in the home or a new and passionate romance a-budding. It might not do to suggest the latter to a settled, thoroughly domesticated, married male subject – not, anyway, if his wife was listening.

Certainly the art of interpreting the cards is easier than palm reading, if only because it is always perfectly clear what the cards *are* – and they do not change. The secret, aside from the play of the intuition, lies in slowly and carefully weighing up the meaning of each card as it is turned over, then equally carefully fitting it into the pattern that the other cards are making. The keyword is *combination*, making each card become a new portion of one story, thoroughly and consistently within the framework of the chosen layout.

Do not be too perturbed if at first the cards come out as a motley, jumbled array of contradictions and confusions; that can happen even to professionals. But in that case do not ever try another reading right away. If you do not wait a full day, preferably seven days, the traditions of cartomancy say that very bad luck will befall you and your subject.

All in all, the skill of card reading (once the basic meanings have been learned) is no more difficult than the skill which allows you to remember the run of cards, and their implications, in games like bridge or poker. Not more difficult, that is, until you feel that you are good enough with the ordinary cards to promote yourself into the first division of fortune telling – by buying yourself a pack of Tarot cards.

TAROT—THE HIGHER OCCULTISM

No one knows the true origins of the Tarot cards, a fact which has stimulated centuries of scholars to produce theories of the most fascinating and unlikely complexity. It may be that some early forms of the cards came into Europe from Arab occultists, or with the westward migrations of the Indo-European forerunners of the Romany people, whom we call gypsies. In any case, the first record of such cards was a pack, numbering seventy-eight, with which fortunes were being told in fourteenth-century Europe.

No doubt, though, that the Tarot is very old and very remarkable. It has become encrusted and encumbered with the most incredible amount of high occult lore, so much so that some occultists insist that it is the repository of *all* occult wisdom, if not indeed the key to all the mysteries of the universe – in, of course, secretly coded, symbolic form. From the Tarot there radiate out associations and interconnections with every other equally complex and symbol-burdened occult system: astrology and alchemy, Gnosticism and Cabbalism, Hindu mysticism and ancient Egyptian magic, hermetics and numerology – these are only a few of them. For those who do not wish to take even a few steps into the twilit and tangled labyrinths of the higher occultism, the Tarot is no place for dabbling.

Or so its users would say – forgetting that in the fourteenth century not only did laymen dabble freely, they also used this mighty and mysterious container of hidden knowledge to play card games, for money. So we may equally dip into the fringes of the Tarot and become acquainted at least with the simpler basics of the seventy-eight cards. They are, after all, the direct ancestors of the cards with which we play bridge and poker – or, so far in this chapter, tell fortunes.

The Tarot has four suits: *cups* (= hearts); *pentacles* or *coins* (= diamonds); *wands* or *batons* (= clubs); *swords* (= spades). They each progress from the ace to the ten, like our cards. But when we come to the court cards there is a difference. There are four kinds of court cards: kings, queens, knaves (sometimes called 'pages') and *knights*. That makes a pack of fifty-six cards, each with its special set of meanings (shown in shortened form on pages 109–113).

But in the old medieval card games there was also a separate group of cards, twenty-two of them, which 'triumphed' over the others in play – a word and a process from which our word 'trump' has descended. And these twenty-two cards are the core of the Tarot's magic, the place where most of that potent occult symbolism is concentrated. They are sometimes called the Greater Trumps, but are more often known as the *Major Arcana,* and the fifty-six cards of the four suits are then the *Minor Arcana.* It is an apt name, if you remember that 'arcane' means secret, mysterious, known only to special initiates.

Translating the Trumps

Whole books can and have been written unravelling the wealth of symbolic meaning attached to any *one* of the Major Arcana. And complexity grows further when we learn that over the centuries many occultists have redesigned and altered the detailed pictorial images on these twenty-two cards, often imposing their own, peculiar occult interests and preferences. Here we will stay with the widely used medieval French pack (in colour, pages 54–55) in order to adhere to early traditions of the Tarot which most later variations used as their starting point. Such packs can still readily be bought, not all that expensively, from shops specialising in occult books and paraphernalia. The following, then, is a very abbreviated note of the symbolic frames of reference for each of the twenty-two, along with the more simplified associations each carries for ready-made fortune telling. The Major Arcana often bear printed numbers as well as designs, and though their order is disputed by scholars, the numbering used here is widely accepted.

1. *Juggler.* This card, sometimes called the Magician, represents the human will, freedom of choice, the factors of intellect, self-determination and understanding that separate the human mind from the brute. The simpler omen for fortune telling: a man entering your life, or a choice to be made.

2. *High Priestess.* Sometimes known as the 'Female Pope', representing wisdom and special knowledge, usually intuitive, sometimes hidden and occult; a link with the unconscious or 'irrational' side of the mind with which women are supposed, in magical tradition, to be more in tune. The simple omen: a women entering your life; some sort of secret.

3. *Empress.* Has much in common with earth mothers and other fertility goddesses, and the ultimate fertility and abundance of Mother Nature herself. Omen: creative action, fruitfulness.

4. *Emperor.* Worldly power and authority; dominating and 'rational' masculine principles. Omen: success; the aid of some powerful influence.

5. *Pope*. Has many of the qualities associated with the real papal personage – embodying divine authority and teaching, intermediary between this world and the next; a spiritual, beneficent, paternal figure. Omen: inspiration, religion, spiritual aid.

6. *Lovers*. Has to do with love and marriage, of course, but also with the inner conflicts born of man's dual nature – reason v passion, flesh v spirit, loyalty v infidelity and so on. Omen: love and marriage.

7. *Chariot*. Travel and change, also the prospect of un-expected news and the likelihood of achievement and success. Omen: the same.

8. *Strength*. An abstract card representing no more than the quality of strength itself, whether spiritual, moral or physical. Some scholars prefer to change the places of this card and the eleventh. Omen: the same.

9. *Hermit*. Solitude and contemplation, also the growth of inner wisdom, or illumination, by some sort of spiritual pilgrimage. Omen: caution is advised.

10. *Wheel of Fortune*. Traditional eastern view of the 'cyclical' nature of things, representing in the Tarot the operations of chance in all of life. Omen: good luck.

11. *Justice*. Another abstract, sometimes transposed with Strength in the numbering, similarly representing itself, with the added qualities of balance and the operation of reason and truth. Omen: the same.

12. *Hanged Man*. One of the most mystifyingly rich of the symbolic cards, generally including some element of self-sacrifice leading to rebirth, renewal. On a less drastic level, a submission to the inner, unconscious areas of one's being in order to emerge altered and enhanced, with new spiritual awareness. Omen: difficulties and pain, a need for endurance.

13. *Death*. What else would be number thirteen? But this

further abstract need not represent only itself, as a finality; it is also an extension of the rebirth/transformation theme, resurrection and renewal. Omen: the same.

14. *Temperance.* Not a warning to drinkers but a sign of moderation, balanced mixtures, control and harmony – especially regarding the proper equilibrium between spiritual and material things. Omen: health, orderliness.

15. *Devil.* An ill-favoured card, representing either an external threat or an upsurge of the evil that exists within all humans, perhaps relating to sexual or aggressive urges, or both. Omen: 'carnality' and the operation of fate.

16. *Tower* (or 'Falling Tower'). Another powerful symbol of misfortune, destruction, loss, ruin, etc. But, as usual in the Tarot, it can carry the positive hope of a phoenix-like rebirth from catastrophe. Omen: the same.

17. *Star.* A pleasant card, bearing messages of hope, likely achievement of worthy desires, unexpected help. Omen: the same.

18. *Moon.* Carries all the traditional non-Tarot associations with the moon, as in astrology (and also in folk belief, where we get terms like 'lunacy' or 'moon-struck'). Strong elements of the irrational and intuitive, with also some changeability and a leaning towards the occult. Omen: fear, darkness, hidden dangers.

19. *Sun.* Quite the opposite, predictably: a symbol of good fortune, success, happiness, 'illumination' and positive achievement. Omen: the same.

20. *Judgment.* The attainment of full spiritual growth and completion, also the abstraction of judgment (being judged) itself. Omen: changes, new beginnings.

21. *World.* Another symbol of completion, of attaining the goal – an ultimate reward, but more on the plane of spiritual than material attainment. Omen: travel, achievement.

ROI DE COUPE

REINE DES COUPES

VALET DE COUPE

CHEVALIER DES COUPES

Court cards of the cups suit of the Tarot's Minor Arcana. King: a fair (complexioned) man, a dominating or successful figure in business, professional or academic life. Queen: a fair woman, domestically inclined but idealistic and artistic in outer life. Knave (or Page): a fair young person of either sex, pleasant and sensitive; possibly also a message. Knight: a fair young man – possibly a lover (for a female subject) or a competitor (for a male).

Pentacles court cards of the Minor Arcana. King: a man of substance and achievement – but with a tinge of ruthlessness or dishonesty. Queen: a wealthy woman; omen of security. Knave: a cautious young person, perhaps introverted; omen of news about finance. Knight: a reliable, upright young man; omen of solidity.

Wands court cards of the Minor Arcana. King: a strong, determined perhaps inflexible dark man. Queen: an attractive dark woman, sophisticated and sexy. Knave: a young person of either sex; encouraging news to come. Knight: a dark young man, strong and sharp-witted; possibly an omen of travels, or losses.

Swords court cards of the Minor Arcana. King: a dark man in a position of power – a judge, a military officer, a government official. Queen: an intelligent dark woman; also, a widow. Knave: a dark young person, possibly a deceiver. Knight: a dark young man of action, even violence; omen of conflict and danger.

Aces of the Tarot's Minor Arcana. Ace of cups: omen of growth, progress, fertility. Of pentacles: prosperity, financial gain. Of wands: new beginnings, advances (sometimes an omen of a birth to come). Of swords: strength, power, authority, positive achievement.

The twenty-second card never bears a number, and can be seen as either 22 or 0, both immensely portentous numbers in numerological mysticisms. It is named *The Fool*, and is the most complex of all the cards. Basically, perhaps, it represents the as yet unshaped spirit of man, replete with all its contradictions, dualities and inner conflicts – male v female, beast v angel, spirit v flesh, good v evil – along with the immense range of potentialities, limitations, strengths and weaknesses that all of us carry. For this reason the Fool is often chosen to be the 'significator' card in some Tarot fortune-telling layouts. (For simple queries, though, or more 'worldly', less mystical readings, a significator can be chosen from the minor arcana court cards, by sex and complexion just as with modern cards.)

The Minor Arcana receive limited ranges of meaning as befits their lower status. Here is a very condensed note on each of those fifty-six cards (remember that there are fourteen in each suit):

Suit of Cups: ace, fertility; two, friend or lover; three, pleasure; four, disappointment; five, a loss but perhaps a legacy; six, remembrance; seven, ambitions; eight, disappointment, change; nine, success; ten, happiness; knave (or page), a rogue, also news; knight, a fair young man, a lover; queen, a fair woman; king, a fair and successful or notable man.

Pentacles: ace, prosperity; two, difficulties; three, achievement; four, wealth; five, hardship; six, gifts, or perhaps losses; seven, business progress; eight, carefulness; nine, financial gain; ten, finances again, and family; knave, a warning; knight, a worthwhile young man; queen, a well-off woman; king: a wealthy and powerful man, but has been called a general ill omen.

Wands: ace, a new start, or a baby; two, good fortune;

three, business gains; four, calm; five, struggles; six, good news; seven, difficulties; eight, progress; nine, obstacles; ten, hardship, perhaps betrayal; knave, a dark young man, a warning; knight, a dark man, a journey; queen, a dark woman, a hopeful omen; king, a powerful dark man, perhaps danger.

Swords: ace, achievement; two, a temporary lull; three, delays and losses; four, setbacks; five, loss, defeat; six, difficulties, travel; seven, ambitions; eight, hardship, illness; nine, sorrow, death; ten, ill luck, defeat; knave, a dark young man, deceit; knight, a soldier, and conflict; queen, a dark woman, perhaps a widow, danger; king, a dark man or a man in authority, troubles.

Manipulating the Tarot

Again, these few pages can only skim surfaces. If you wish to dabble in the Tarot on that basis, however, a few things must be remembered. First, the cards are not double-headed – some readers state that when a card appears upside down its symbolic meaning (and simple omen) will be *reversed*. So the Falling Tower would become success rather than ruin, and so on. More modern Tarot readers, though, are tending to drop this practice, and to react to the cards as they come, whichever way up. You may make your own choice.

Further, the cards relate to one another in many sub-groupings. Clearly there is something of a progression in the Major Arcana from the material side of things to the spiritual; so some cards have more to do with the outer world, others with the inner, some with the equilibrium between both. Some cards also can be grouped as references to influences upon you (authority, outer circumstances) while others form a group referring to what is happening within you.

More of these interrelations within the pack will no doubt occur to you as you familiarise yourself with the cards. And familiarity is a basic recommendation by all experts: it is essential. Buy the pack that appeals most to you in design and fascination; keep it with you, handle it often, sleep with it under your pillow, spread the cards out and muse on them with your imagination and intuition and receptivity wide open. And do not let anyone else touch them. Ignore those writers who suggest, as with ordinary cards, that the subject should shuffle and cut before a reading. Other hands, it is as often said, will blur the finely tuned 'vibrations' set up between the reader and his or her own cards. Merely let the subject stare concentratedly at them, fixed on the query or problem that is most central at that time, while you shuffle and deal.

As for layouts, you can use some of those outlined for the modern pack, to begin with, and look forward to the day when you are expert enough (and occultist enough) to try the renowned *Tree of Life* layout illustrated opposite. Certainly every good professional has a favourite layout that he or she uses most of the time – except for special occasions or unusual purposes. One of the most popular requires twenty-one cards selected at random (see page 118).

First you remove the Fool or some other significator. Spread out the pack face down and let the subject select the twenty-one cards (by indicating, not touching). Remove those cards and deal them out (face down, right to left) in three rows of seven cards each. That of course will also make seven *vertical* rows of three cards each.

These trios each refer to a specific aspect of the reading, and are considered one at a time, starting on the far right – where the three cards in that row will display the subject's inner state of mind and being. The next trio of cards picture

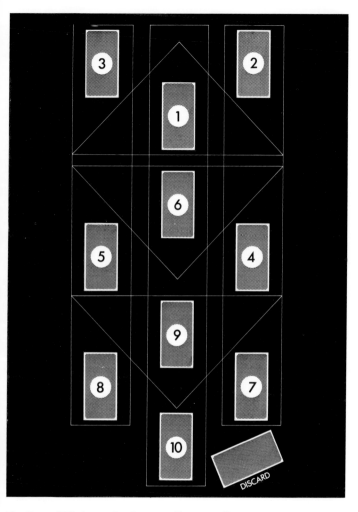

The Tree of Life layout for Tarot reading uses all seventy-eight cards and demands a thorough and intimate knowledge of the pack, with its special symbolism in the vertical and horizontal rows and other interrelationships. Cards are numbered in order of deal, most readers preferring to deal each set of seven at once.

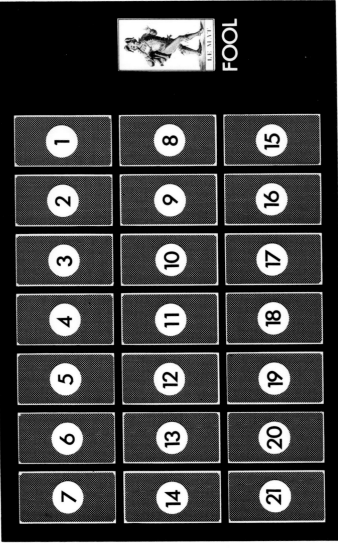

Tarot layout using 21 cards, numbered in order of deal

his home life; the third trio, his hopes and ambitions, or some specific question. The fourth trio indicates what the subject expects will happen as regards his hopes or his question; the fifth shows what may happen that he does *not* expect. The sixth gives a glimpse of his immediate future, and the seventh, on the far left, shows more of the future – either broadly, or in the specific context of the question that has been put.

A special way to focus the Tarot on a single question needs even fewer cards. Again remove a significator, shuffle, then turn up the first ten cards one after another. The first reveals the general circumstances and tendencies affecting the question. The second shows the forces opposing a favourable outcome. The third shows the roots of the problem. The fourth shows some influence that has affected the problem in the past; the fifth shows an influence that has just begun to affect it; the sixth shows an influence that will affect it in future. The seventh reveals the subject's worries on this matter; the eighth shows the roles of his family and friends regarding it; the ninth shows his positive hopes and desires concerning it. And the tenth spells out the answer – how the problem will be resolved.

In a variant of this layout, after the Fool (only him) is removed as significator and the pack shuffled, cut the pack leftwards three times while the subject concentrates hard on the question to be looked into. Then put the pack to-gether and peel off the first twelve cards. Put the Fool in among these twelve and reshuffle them before dealing them out, face *up*, in a row from right to left. The secret of this layout lies in the position of the Fool after the deal. Cards to the right of the Fool concern aspects of importance to the question asked; but cards to the Fool's *left* introduce another question, a 'supplementary', so to speak – one that follows

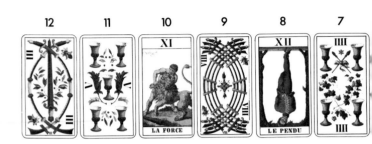

Tarot layout with 12 cards, dealt right to left

naturally from the first and that redefines or subtly alters the answers to be given. (For instance: the subject may have presented the commonplace question 'Will I marry the one I love?'; but the cards may present unexpected supplementaries that he or she ought to have asked, such as 'Will I marry *anyone*?' or 'If so, will I *stay* married, or be happy?')

In this layout, if the Fool comes out as the first card dealt, then the original question has no real importance and it is the hidden supplementary question that must be recognised and confronted. Equally, if the Fool falls at the end of the deal, far left, then there is no hidden supplementary, no considered offshoots of the original question.

~imately, it will be up to the individual whether he or she

FOOL   5   4   3   2   1

LE MAT.   LA MORT   L'EMPEREUR   L'ÉTOILE

wishes to pursue the glamorous symbolisms of the Tarot any further into the shadowy realms of mysticism and magic. If so, this much simplified introduction will need amplifying by the subtle and learned tomes of the scholars (towards which I might recommend standard works by A. E. Waite and Alfred Douglas, or sensible modern writers like Richard Cavendish and Bill Butler). Otherwise, those who wish merely to peer for a moment inside the multicoloured mysteries of the Tarot will find much to enthral them even on short acquaintance – and may then return to fortune telling with their ordinary cards, to find that whole new extensions of their meanings may have been opened up, thanks to the echoes and resonances of the Tarot.

lipse of the sun – a random omen traditionally warning of large-scale misfortune.

The
Future at Random

Fortune telling is really nothing more than the reading of *omens*, and the various systems and techniques are merely ways of locating the omens and recording their meanings. But omen-reading takes us back to the most primitive and basic roots of fortune telling, which for all its great age still exists in the commonest superstition and folk belief. At the root is the flat statement that if *this* happens, *that* will surely follow – a one-to-one 'causal' connection. So superstition tells us that if a black cat crosses our path, we are in luck (or out of luck if we happen to be Americans); that sunshine on a wedding day assures a happy marriage; that an itchy nose means company coming, and so on. We all know such omens – many of us believe in some of them.

Such omens are based on *randomly* occurring events. We do not go looking for black cats, nor can we contrive sunny wedding days or itchy noses. And this kind of natural randomness lies at the very core of systems like astrology and palmistry, for neither do we contrive the positions of the stars or the wrinkles on our hands.

Yet there are some kinds of fortune telling that use randomness but that also involve some effort on the part of the fortune teller, as the instigator of the random events. Card reading is one such: *you* shuffle and deal, though the cards fall as they will. And other kinds of 'contrived randomness' ought to be a part of the armoury of a self-taught fortune teller – most especially, perhaps, the homely practice of reading *tea leaves*.

A CUPFUL OF FATE

The preparations for tea leaf reading could hardly be simpler. You merely make a pot of tea. Use an ordinary brand of loose Indian tea with relatively substantial leaves, and pour yourself a cup – into a plain cup, no patterns, and, of course, no strainer. Let the leaves settle, then pour off most of the tea. Swirl the residue round in the cup to disperse the leaves, then quickly invert the cup over a saucer. Turn it up again, and the wet leaves should be adhering over much of the cup's inner surface.

If you wish, you may inject a little magic into the process: swirl the cup a special three or seven times, and swirl it in the 'sunwise' (clockwise) direction preferred in white magic. In any event, the scattered smears and clusters of leaves will await your interpretive attention.

If there are a great many leaves left in the cup, the subject of the reading will lead a rich, full life, and has a generous nature tending to the emotional. Perhaps an unusual amount of leaves will take these qualities to the extreme, indicating a complex and jumbled life full of self-indulgence. Conversely, a thin and limited scattering of leaves signifies a controlled, logical person with a tidy and organised life – tending, at its extreme, to be a trifle cold and over-disciplined.

The cup's inside surface where the handle is joined represents the subject's personal life and home – so any recognisable shapes found in this region will pertain to those areas of the life. The subject might keep the handle pointing to himself or herself, which offers a time distinction: leaves to the left of the handle refer to the subject's past, those to the right refer to the future. Alternatively, you can see time in the vertical areas: leaves nearest the rim have to do with the immediate present, those nearest the bottom with the distant future.

Leaves actually on the bottom of the cup indicate ill luck; their shapes specify the forms of this misfortune. If a drop or two of tea can be discerned there, too, they represent symbolic 'tears' and foretell sadness. Any perceptible letters of the alphabet are the initials of persons who will be important to the subject – directly and personally if the initials are near the handle, otherwise more remotely.

Three small leaves together signify the entrance of some man into the subject's life; two small leaves mean a woman; a considerable number of very small leaves, a child or children. Small dots foretell the coming of money; straight lines mean some progress; circles mean completion of some current intention or hope.

Other typical shapes that can be looked for are pictured on pages 126–127. Some may not be instantly recognisable, but do not let that worry you. A very little experience will enable you easily to see shapes in the leaves, especially if – as always – you set your imagination and intuition free, letting the associations and ideas come as they will. Do not lose heart if no clear shapes appear at first glance; turn the cup round and round, gaze at it from different angles, concentrate first on separate small clusters, until the first sparks of recognition are struck. But even if absolutely nothing resembles any shape you have ever seen, so that the whole cup is a chaotic and meaningless smear, it may not be the fault of your perceptions: it may be that your subject's life is in a chaotic muddle, and the leaves reflect it. In that case, abandon the reading, and wait at least seven days before trying again.

If you dislike tea and have none in the house, you may use

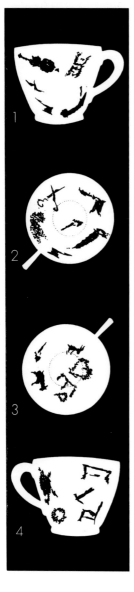

Sample tea-leaf shapes, to accustom the novice to picking out recognizable forms. **Cup 1:** at the top, a clear *violin* shape, sign of individuality. To its right, possibly a letter H (*initials* refer to people in the subject's life, and their position within the cup indicate the importance) or perhaps a *ladder*, omen of success and advancement. Below the violin, a winged shape – either a *bird*, usually a good omen, or a *bat*, a sign of possible betrayal. Lower left, possibly an *axe*, meaning labour rewarded. Next to it, a vague shape that might be a *comet*, meaning a visitor coming from afar, or perhaps a *root*, meaning secrets. **Cup 2:** just to the left of the handle, an undefined *cloud*, meaning unresolved difficulties (in the subject's past). Next to it, *scissors*, omen of separation. Next, a shape like a steaming *cooking pot*, or a smoking *cooker*, warning of domestic difficulties. Below it, a *saw*, a warning to beware of strangers. Then the *axe* shape again (see cup 1), to the right (the near future) of the handle. At the bottom of the cup, a shape like an old *pistol*, hinting at dangers and problems to come, a strong omen of ill luck. **Cup 3:** the *pistol* shape again (see cup 2), in this position an omen of dangers in the near future. Two animal shapes here – on the left, what looks like a *goat*, a sign of enemies near; on the right, near the handle, the vague shape of a *donkey*, sign of peace and contentment. A clear *initial* E in this cup (see cup 1), flanked by two vague *triangle* shapes, good omens if the apex is visibly pointing upwards. (But they might also refer to children, perhaps connected to the person whose initial is 'E'.) **Cup 4:** next to the handle, the shape perhaps of a *tortoise* (turn the picture round and round when working out the forms), sign of a sensitive nature. At the top, an obvious *table*, omen of a happy occasion. Below it, perhaps a *pickaxe*, meaning hard work to do, or an *anchor*, an omen of success. Bottom right, a clear *chair* shape, a sign of better times. And lastly a *circle*, a success omen – though it could be taken as a *ball* or sphere, a warning of changes to come. **Cup 5:** the shape at the top left might be a potted *plant* (a good omen, especially if flowering) or perhaps a sailing *ship*, omen of good news or a journey. To its right, a *rabbit* or *hare*, meaning a timid nature. Next to the handle at the top, possibly some long-billed bird like a *stork*, a sign of happiness. Below it, a shape like a child's drawing of a *house*, a good omen. Next to it, the *scissors* shape again (see cup 2). Below that, a small *cup* or *pot*, suggesting a good deed to be done. And to its right, a *leaf* shape, omen of news to come. **Cup 6:** just to the left of the handle, a puzzling shape that might be the head of an *animal* (if a *dog*, a sign of faithfulness). Above it, a spindly, almost giraffe-like shape that is more likely an upside-down *fork* or *trident*, a warning to be cautious. At the top, possibly a bulky piece of *furniture* on short legs (a sign of domestic peace) or an upside-down *bowl* or some other container, a sign of pleasant happenings. To its right, an inverted *triangle*, a bad omen. Below it, an *eye*, a hint to be wary, next to an inverted *glass* or *chalice*, a sign of firm friendship. At the right of the handle, the *comet* (or *root*) shape again (see cup 1). On the bottom of the cup, a (fir) *tree* shape, sign of achievement, and a small shape that might be the numeral *1* (not a good omen in this position) or, inverted, a *nail*, a sign of enmity. **Cup 7:** Here on the bottom of the cup is the *chalice* shape again (see cup 6), not so happy an omen in this position, with a vague *cross* shape that warns of illness. Near the handle is a *dagger* or *sword*, warning of strong emotionalism, and a crawling *insect*, suggesting worries. Plain *lines*, below that, signify advancement. Next to them, the *goat* shape again (see cup 3), and above it a *star*, an excellent omen of good luck. Above it, perhaps some kind of fruit like a *pear*, a sign of financial good luck. **Cup 8:** Next to the handle, what seems to be a teapot or *kettle*, an omen of domestic bliss in this position (it would mean domestic upheaval on the opposite side of the cup). At the top, what may be a small *ship* (see cup 5) or perhaps some form of luggage or *handbag*, an omen of travel. The next rather obscure shape might be a low, wide-branching *tree* (good omen, as in cup 6) or some (upside-down) headgear, even a *crown*, a success omen. Below it, even more obscure, may be some sort of utensil with a handle, like a *jug*, which is a warning to follow only good influences. There are two vague *circle* shapes here again, both excellent omens, and all the more so with the recurrence of that extremely strong omen of good fortune, the *star*.

coffee grounds for divination just as easily. Many of the shapes and meanings given for tea leaves apply to coffee too, but there are some special factors. Make your unstrained cup of black coffee but pour it slowly on to a white plate, swirling the plate to let the coffee spill over the edge and the grounds disperse. And look for some special shapes in coffee: a square means joy, a triangle means unexpected good fortune, a circle with a dot or dots means a baby coming, a wavy line foretells a journey.

THE BOOK OF CHANGES

To move from looking for fate in the dregs of a cuppa to seeking the future in the serene oriental subtlety of the world's oldest book is surely moving from the faintly ridiculous to the nearly sublime. But no fortune teller's shelves should be without the ancient Chinese *I Ching*, known as the 'Book of Changes', which takes divination on to quite another plane. It goes beyond reciting rote meanings, beyond even the labyrinthine occultism of the Tarot, reaching towards the airy realms of eastern mysticism and poetry – all in a quite useable but, yes, inscrutable package.

The *I Ching* (pronunciation is contested, but is generally said to be rather like EE KING) is not really a fortune teller's manual; it is a repository of the wisdom of Chinese sages and philosophers some thousands of years ago. It is cloudy with symbolism, enigmatic with aphorism, resonant with elusive meaning that seems always on the threshold of being enormously illuminating. Yet it has always been used as a mechanism for divination, performed in a simple way that uses the randomness principle.

In fact it is the highest form of *bibliomancy*, the use of books for divination. Among the lower forms is the practice of letting a Bible fall open at random and placing a finger or

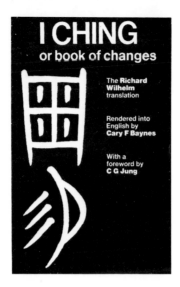

I CHING
or book of changes

The **Richard Wilhelm** translation

Rendered into English by **Cary F Baynes**

With a foreword by **C G Jung**

pin also at random on to a page – where an 'omen' will emerge from the verse thus selected. The *I Ching* similarly directs you to a specific part of the book in random fashion. Originally the Chinese used a handful of yarrow stalks, which they cast and arranged in complex ways, to find their place in the book. Today, more simply, you need merely toss up three coins six separate times, and from this you achieve a symbolic shape called a 'hexagram'.

The hexagrams are figures made up of six horizontal lines, either broken or unbroken, one above the other. These are the keys to the *I Ching*, each section of which explains one of the sixty-four possible hexagrams. It works like this:

The first toss of the three coins comes up, let us say, two heads and a tail. The book tells you that this gives an 'unchanging broken line', thus: —— ——. This is the bottom line of your hexagram; it builds upwards. The next toss gives you, say, three heads – a 'changing unbroken line':

129

————. Next, two tails and a head, an 'unchanging un-broken line': ————. Next, three tails, obviously a 'changing broken line': —— ——. The next throw necessarily must be one of those four again, say another two heads and a tail: —— ——. And the final throw could be, say, another three heads: ————. So you have your hexagram.

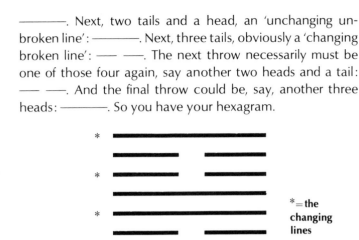

*= the changing lines

You will have perhaps been puzzled by the 'unchanging' or 'changing' parts of those descriptions. This refers to the fact that by throwing the coins for one hexagram you have actually achieved *two* – because the so-called 'changing' lines can be turned into their opposites, to give a second hexagram and so a second reading from the book. But first we must attend to the original hexagram.

You look it up in the *I Ching*'s chart and are directed to the appropriate section of the book. There you learn that your hexagram is called *Ku* and bears the general title 'Work after Spoiling'. There you will read a number of terse, concise and rather enigmatic statements under two main headings. The first heading is 'The Symbol' and begins: 'Wind blowing around the foot of the mountain/ Symbolises Work after Spoiling'. The other heading is The Judgment and states: 'Work after Spoiling. Great Success. It is of benefit to cross the great water.'

Even more comments of similar vagueness follow. But if you have one of the good English translations of the *I Ching*

130

(by Richard Wilhelm or by the American Da Liu) there will be a most welcome commentary, which will elucidate the cryptic comments. In the case of our sample, it will suggest that 'Work after Spoiling' may generally refer to a bad time coming to an end and giving way, with a little effort, to good times – and that rethinking, introducing new ways of looking at things or doing things, will bring rewards.

Still within the hexagram 'Ku', there are omens attached to each line. Our sample is said to have 'six at the bottom': 'six' is the term used, mystifyingly, for a broken line, and this one means that there may be some danger. The next line up is 'nine in the second place' (and 'nine' is always the word for an unbroken line), which is more reassuring, telling us not to be too overanxious about the work that is necessary after the spoiling. And so on – with, thankfully, comments from the book's translator shedding light on these aphorisms as on the others.

But we still have not finished, for now it is time to make the book live up to its sub-title by going through the changes. Remember that our original hexagram had three 'changing lines'. These must now be turned into their opposites, broken becoming unbroken and vice versa. Our new

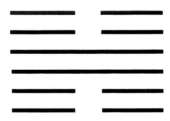

hexagram is looked up as before, to act as something of a supplementary divination to the first. It is called *Hsiao Kuo*, or 'Slight Excess' – and it tells us, among other things, that 'it is not good to go up; it is good to stay below' and (from the bottom line) 'A bird encounters misfortune when it soars'. There are a good few documented modern cases of people changing their minds about planned airplane trips, after receiving this hexagram, and being glad of it when disaster overtook the plane.

Because the *I Ching*'s editors do such an able job of clarifying the mysteries, there is no need to delve further here into the book. But two points need stressing. First, the book *is* a repository of wisdom – that sort of 'mysticism' which tends towards philosophy, towards a balanced and aware view of man and his place in the world, rather than towards dubious occult knowledge. Indeed, *balance* is the keyword of the *I Ching*: it is informed throughout by the essential Chinese view of the *yang* and the *yin*, representing the archetypal 'opposites' that are at the core of the mysteries of the universe (day/night, male/female, good/evil,

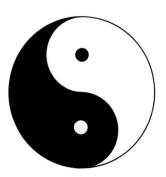

The ancient symbol of the yin and the yang – representing the conjunction and balance of opposites.

etc.) and of the dual nature of man. It leads to the view that harmony, equilibrium, balance, is the most desirable and essential state – the 'reconciliation of opposites'. And of course the principle of opposites is behind the central pattern of the book's 'changes'.

So the I Ching ought not to be seen as an oriental oddity or an amusing party game. Indeed, the tradition says that the book may react on you if you take it too lightly, giving you a hexagram that is either mocking or unsettling. Instead, approach the book with respect, if not even reverence. You may consult it over a specific question: it will not matter even if the question is fairly trivial, like 'should I take my plane trip?' as long as it is important to you and asked seriously.

When throwing the three coins, shake them quietly in your cupped hands and focus your mind on your question, or your general state of being if that is what you want to be illuminated, excluding all other thoughts. And when you have your hexagram, read it and re-read it and ponder over it. Here is the second important point to remember: the Chinese sages said that the I Ching sets up 'echoes in the mind'. It does not directly foretell the future; it opens doors for your own subjective perceptions of what may potentially happen. After all, if you have a question to ask, you may already be able to guess or suspect much of the answer, or have feelings one way or the other. The I Ching's wisdom articulates those feelings. It brings to the surface your unconscious awareness of possibilities.

So the 'echoes in your mind' that it creates are ways of tuning yourself in on your own unconscious being, your intuitions, your own nature, with all its potential for directing your own life pattern. The object is to bring you to a greater knowledge of yourself, and thereby to a harmonious balance, your *yang* and *yin* in serene and fruitful equilibrium. Remember that the ancient Chinese used the book primarily for spiritual guidance. They would be as offended by its use for light-hearted fortune telling as a modern vicar might be by someone who used the Bible merely to stick pins in, for omens.

ADDING UP FORTUNES

The art of *numerology* is probably not as old as the Book of Changes, but it has something of a pedigree. The ancient Greek mystics like Pythagoras developed it to its highest – establishing that just about anything, from the qualities of a person to the secrets of the universe, can be expressed (or found) in numbers. Over the centuries, much symbolic association became attached to simple numbers, and today these associations have become established as the usual, standard references for fortune telling.

Putting aside the mysticisms of antiquity, the process becomes laughably simple for anyone who can add. Only the numbers 1 to 9 need really be worried about, because all other numbers are usually reduced to single digits by left-to-right addition. So 11 becomes $1 + 1 = 2$, and 1978 becomes $1 + 9 + 7 + 8 = 25$, which goes on to become $2 + 5 = 7$. There is not much more to it than that.

The rote meanings of the simple numbers have humanised references – the sorts of people to which each corresponds – and generalised. So *One*, as befits the first of all numbers, relates to dominant, aggressive, creative, powerful people. They tend to be energetic, inventive, individualistic but born leaders, ambitious; they might also be self-centred, ruthless, obsessionally single-minded. They make tycoons, military leaders, scientific discoverers, artistic innovators, pioneers, who channel their energy into their chosen vocations rather than into their relationships or the quality of their lives.

In general terms, then, One is the number of creative energy, discovery, the finding of new paths.

One links traditionally with astrology's over-masculine sun, and in the same way *Two* goes to similar extremes with femininity (the moon). Two refers to passive, retiring persons, not the leaders but the led. They will have charm, tact, sensitivity and intuitive awareness; they may also suffer from insecurity and feelings of inferiority. And age-old male chauvinism also links Two with forces of darkness and the occult – the serpent as well as Eve.

Three is a good number to have, for its people blend some creative energy, individuality and drive with tempered qualities of charm, attractiveness and an articulate, lively ability to get on with people. They can be clever, talented, enjoyable people to whom success comes easily, though they may also be shallow, showy, self-indulgent, even deceitful. In general there is much sexuality in Three but also much spirituality (it is the number of the Holy Trinity).

Four is related to its most common natural occurrences, the seasons and the directions, and so is an 'earthbound' number. Four is also the number of the sides of a square, which is an apt description of its people. They too are earthbound, rather dull, staid and plodding, unimaginative and resistant to change, though practical, hard-working and enduring. Not a pleasant number, Four, offering little hope of ready success and every chance of poor luck and a comparatively hard life.

Five moves to the other extreme, not plodding but too lively, given to nervous tension, impulsiveness, quick temper, changeable to the point of being erratic. Such people enjoy adventure and novelty but are easily bored; sexuality is important in their lives, fidelity hardly at all. They may be brilliant, but will be jacks-of-all-trades rather than concentratedly excellent at one. Their lively, restless energies make them attractive, and they can face up to obstacles and adversity, but reliability is not really their strongest point.

Six, in the old symbolisms, is a 'perfect number', the perfection of balance, harmony, completeness. Its people too are well balanced, with the virtues of loyalty, stamina and determination, and a special gift for faithfulness in love and domestic bliss. They might succumb to a smug and blinkered self-satisfaction and a fixation on the *status quo,* but they are likely to know happiness and fulfilment.

Seven is one of the most potent numbers in mysticism, because so many things in the universe come in groups of seven, or multiples. It tends to be an unworldly, spiritual number, and its people are equally unworldly, inclined towards quiet, philosophical pursuits. They may be intellectually gifted, but not communicative; they keep to themselves, musing and meditating. So they risk loneliness and unhappiness, but they may find a special peace of their own.

Eight has some of the qualities of Four – certainly the solidity and tenacity and some of the resilience. But the people of Eight are fighters, pulling themselves up by their bootstraps, tough and efficient seekers after success and power. They might be obsessive about material things, and their ambitions might take them beyond the edge of propriety or legality now and then. But they never give up, they are their own masters and they deserve respect.

Nine is another especially symbolic mystic number, relating to ultimate completion and highest spiritual attainment. Its people are achievers – brilliant, inspired, strong-willed – whose work is full of humanitarianism, high idealism and selflessness. They can be great teachers or creators or benefactors, full of courage and love for their fellow man, with a risk otherwise of being woolly-minded, eccentric dreamers with no practicality whatsoever.

Despite the usual practice of reducing numbers to the single digits, there are a few special larger numbers which are singled out for attention by mystically minded numerologists, and these can help to fill out the picture for the fortune teller. *Eleven*, for one, relates to special mystic awarenesses and to the spirit of self-sacrifice, towards a movement on to a high plane of perception and spiritual being. *Twelve* is impressively symbolic of completeness, wholeness, coming full circle to something near perfection (like the twelve months, zodiac signs, days of Christmas, apostles, etc.).

Thirteen, being one more than the perfect Twelve, tips over into something rather like sacrilege, and so is traditionally the number of ill luck and the blackest magical arts. *Twenty-two* brings in again a mystic sense of wholeness and completion (the twenty-two cards in the Tarot's Major Arcana) while *Forty* is an equally potent number of fullness and completion.

But back with the plain single-digit numbers, the way to put these into action for fortune telling is almost banally straightforward. Using one of the common sets of number-letter equivalents (see page 138) you can work out the 'ruling number' for almost anything. Commonly it is performed on a birth date – say, the one we used in Chapter One to work out a horoscope, 16 September 1949. You already have numbers for the day and the year, so you need merely find the equivalents for the month. In September's case they are $1+5+7+2+5+4+2+5+9=40=4+0=4$. So the overall birth-date number is added up thus: $1+6$ (the day) $+4$ (the month) $+1+9+4+9$ (the year) $=34=3+4=7$.

So Seven is the number of this person. But if he or she

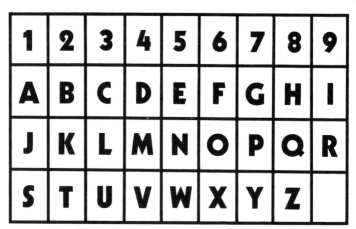

A widely used system of number-letter equivalents

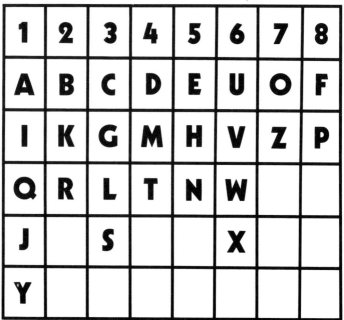

Another common system, omitting the mystic number 9

does not care for those associations, there are other ways. Use, instead, the normal number equivalent for a month – 9 for September, the ninth month. The sum becomes $1+6+9+1+9+4+9=39=3+9=12=1+2=3$. So now he or she is a Three person. And even then there are different approaches, especially the use of the *name*.

Try it with your own name, and the number equivalents of the letters. Perhaps you will not care for the number that you reach first time. Never mind: John Smith might not care for the number of his name, but he can recall that he signs his cheques 'J. E. Smith' and can try that variant. (The number he gets then will represent his most formal, outer self, the image he wishes to present to the world.) Or he can recall that his friends call him Johnny or Jack, and can try that. (Then he will get a number for his true, inner self, known to loved ones and good friends.)

It is obvious where the 'randomness' comes in. Few of us have much control over our names; none has control over the date of birth. But the technique can be used beyond one's own self. Try it on the city or town you live in. Or on the place you are going for your next holiday. Or on your beloved's name, or the firm you work for, or a horse you might bet on. . . The possibilities are endless. Ideally, if your ruling number is Three, you should live in a Three city, bet on a Three horse, do important things on a Three day. The third day of the month will be lucky for you, as will a third month and a Three year (wait till 1983 for the next one).

For more variations, try adding up the number equivalents of only the vowels in the name of someone, to learn the special, inner nature of the name's owner. It works for cities too: the vowels of Paris add up to sexy, feminine Two. If a person's birth-date number clashes badly with his or her name number, no matter how many approaches you use, it may be because there are unresolved conflicts and personal struggles going on within that person. And if one number does not appear at all in any of the equivalents of a person's name, birthday and so on, then the person is entirely lacking – in the personality – all the qualities of that number.

RANDOM SCATTERINGS

All sorts of other systems using the randomness principle can be pursued, if the fortune teller feels that even those discussed so far do not offer enough variety. But that pursuit is likely to lead to an array of systems which are either limited to the point of dullness or fanciful to the point of silliness.

As a temporary change from cards, for instance, one might plunder the Monopoly or backgammon set for its *dice* and roll random fortunes with them. Most users like to mark out a circle (one American expert's insistence on chalk drawn on velvet need not be religiously followed) and roll the dice into the circle. Only a little practice is needed to enable you to hit the circle most of the time – but it is quite satisfactory even if you miss. You use three dice (rolled from a cup, also as in backgammon) and the standard meanings of the various possible numbers, from three to eighteen, appear on pages 142–143. If one die fails to enter the circle, read the omen of the number made by the other two, but add that the one left out foretells that your best-laid plans will go awry. Two dice out of the circle warn of trouble and strife. Three dice out suggest not only that the thrower was short on accuracy but that a wish will come true – though not with entirely the desired consequences.

There are one or two mildly interesting variations on the dice theme, but with only those few numbers to look for the interest of this system may soon pall. For British readers who still enjoy traditional pub games, *dominoes* may provide a brief respite – but only brief, again, for there are a mere twenty-eight pieces in a set of dominoes, each one has a simple, standard meaning, and that is all there is to it. (See pages 144–145.) You may try a few variants – for instance, the meaning can be said to be reversed if a domino emerges upside down. So if a piece that has five at the top and three at the bottom means a visitor, if it appears on the table with the three at the top and the five at the bottom it could mean a departure.

Otherwise there are some amusing little games that children like to use for party-piece fortune telling – like suspending a ring from a thread and dangling it over a container (perhaps a glass). Ask it a question: and if it moves to strike the right side of the container (and has not been obviously swung by the holder) the answer is yes, or the omen is good, while the left side is no, or bad. In the same vein, tie thread around the middle of a needle so that it hangs horizontally. When it is still, ask the question; if it begins to spin clockwise (round to the right) the answer is yes, and leftwards is the opposite. Sometimes the needle may be held over the wrist or heart of the subject to 'foretell' whether he or she will marry (spinning right is yes, left is no) or, in the case of a girl, how many children of which sex she will have (revolutions right show the number of boys, revolutions left the girls, no spin at all means childlessness).

And if all that seems both pointless and trivial, it is certainly no worse than a system now happily obsolete which relied on a hungry chicken. Mark out a sizeable circle on the ground, write the letters of the alphabet round it and drop a few seeds or kernels of corn on each letter. Then place the chicken in the middle, and read your omen from the un-doubtedly meaningless order of letters at which it pecks. If the bird does not eat at all, the omen is disastrous.

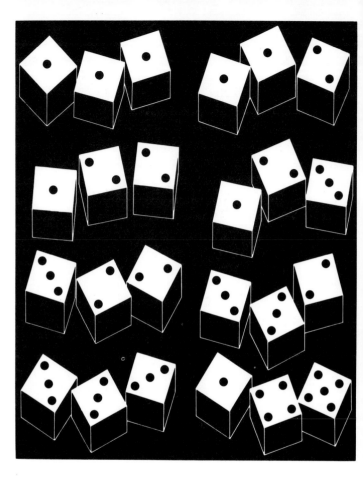

Traditional meanings of the possible throws that can be made with three dice. (These are said to hold true however the total is made up – i.e. an eight is an eight whether you have thrown a six and two ones or a four, three and one or whatever.) Three – a surprise on its way. Four – ill luck threatens. Five – make a wish and it will come true. Six – misfortune and loss. Seven – danger ahead in business or money matters. Eight –

beware outside influence. Nine – a marriage in the offing. Ten – a birth. Eleven – departure of a loved one. Twelve – good news on its way. Thirteen – sadness in the offing. Fourteen – a good friend will aid you. Fifteen – be on guard against setbacks. Sixteen – travel and enjoyment will come your way. Seventeen – some rethinking and reorganisation will occur. Eighteen – good fortune, success, happiness.

Fortunes can be told with dominoes merely by drawing and interpreting one or more – i.e. reeling off the standard meaning. (Some seers say that the meaning is reversed if the domino comes upside down – but others dispense with this extra complication.) Six-six: success, prosperity. Six-five: status being enhanced. Six-four: a beneficial change. Six-three: travel, enjoyment. Six-two: improved circumstances. Six-one: a good friend. Six-blank: use extra caution. Five-five: extra money coming. Five-four: good fortune. Five-three: news, or a guest. Five-two: sociability,

enjoyment. Five-one: a love relationship. Five-blank: sadness. Four-four: happiness. Four-three: domestic difficulties. Four-two: losses, setbacks. Four-one: money troubles. Four-blank: bad news, obstacles. Three-three: a wedding in the offing. Three-two: money troubles. Three-one: something unexpected. Three-blank: surprises. Two-two: enemies, betrayal. Two-one: difficulties. Two-blank: serious difficulties. One-one: pleasure, enjoyment. One-blank: good news. Double blank: dire ill omen.

All
In the Mind

'To sleep, perchance to dream.' But Hamlet had it wrong, for modern experiments have shown that just as we all sleep, so too we all dream – every night, for some of the time – whether we remember it or not. Indeed, some scientists think that we sleep *in order to* dream: that dreaming plays some vital role in keeping our psychic machinery tuned up and ticking over. Just how and why, they do not yet know. But our primitive ancestors, and the ancients of long-dead civilisations, had their own answers. They were certain that dreams were supernatural messages – from the gods, the spirits, the demons – bearing news of what was to come.

For as long as written records have been kept, so records of prophetic dreams have been included. Of course, the messages needed some unravelling: gods and oracles tend to speak cryptically at the best of times. So, also throughout history, there have been interpreters of dreams – often important personages at the courts of monarchs, whose dreams were of huge significance to the future of the entire state. Remember Daniel, in the Bible, interpreting Nebuchad-nezzar's dream in Babylon – or Joseph doing the same for the Pharaoh of Egypt? Equally there were interpreters at hand for the VIP dreams in ancient India, China, Assyria, Greece, Rome. . .

When it came to Rome, though, a clever seer named Artemidorus, in the second century A.D., realised that dream

146

Aliens – important changes coming

'messages' were as important to the man in the street as to the Emperor. So he compiled a comprehensive catalogue of commonplace dream symbols and their 'meanings' – the first dream book. And through the centuries hordes of scholars have adapted and expanded his work into libraries full of lists and indexes and dictionaries of interpreted dreams.

The advantages of fortune telling by dreams will be clear. No paraphernalia, no arithmetic, no complex systems: just listen to someone's dream and pluck out the omen. What could be simpler?

Bees – omen of good fortune, prosperity

You might, of course, complicate matters a little if you grow tired of reciting the standard meanings and seek to introduce elements of, say, modern Freudian or Jungian psychoanalysis, which of course uses dream interpretation in a far more sophisticated and demanding manner (and for different purposes). But for the present, your starting place must be the exceedingly straightforward and standardised meanings of dream images. Remember, though, all those mountains of written material: this chapter can be a catalogue only of a limited sampling of dream symbols.

And first, a general principle or two might be mentioned. Many interpretations follow the principle usually called *association* – the obvious sort of one-to-one connection between image and meaning. A dream of falling, which all of us have had at some time, means a 'downward' trend in fortunes, a definite decline and fall. (Other parts of the dream, or other dreams, may clarify just where in one's life this decline will set in.) Any sort of ascent – up stairs, ladders, mountains, etc. – is a good omen, any descent is bad. A dream of flying means 'soaring ambition' (again, look to other images to show whether the ambition will be fulfilled or frustrated). And the dream of being unable to run from some danger warns of a threat approaching, or a lack of inner strength to cope with adversity.

But just to confuse things a little, dream interpretation also makes much use of the principle of *opposition*. That very common dream of appearing nude or semi-nude in public is in fact a good omen, of financial gain or happiness

Chains – good omen, an end to problems

in love. A dream of a frightful monster equally means good luck and happiness on the way. And a dream of facing or struggling against some immovable obstacle means quite the contrary – that obstacles will be overcome.

Now, though, we can look at our catalogue of dreams and meanings, as full as space will allow.

A to Z of Dreams

Abandonment. If you abandon someone important to you, ill luck coming. If you are abandoned, an end to present difficulties.

Abduction. If yourself, you will defeat enemies. If someone else, unexpected news will arrive.

Abyss. If you avoid it, you will overcome your troubles. If you fall in, financial troubles coming.

Crime – yours, success; another's, a beneficial change

Devil – beware enemies, temptations

Acting. Yourself on stage: be strong against temporary setback. Others acting: a journey (also a warning against gossiping).

Adultery. If you commit it: beware of new friends. If you are merely tempted: a rich life foretold.

Angel. Success, happiness, prosperity.

Anger. Directed at a friend: someone will aid you. At a stranger: unexpected good news.

Artist. Usually a painter; a warning to change your life pattern. If you are the artist: a danger of failure. If you are the model: a danger of treachery.

Assault. If you were assaulted: useful news to come. If others: beware slander.

Drunkenness – yours, a warning; another's, a loss

Aunt. Good omen of beneficial influences (as is true of dreams of other relatives). Visiting an aunt: a legacy.

Baby. An ill omen if the infant is very young, and worse if it is ill. Seeing a baby born: unhappiness coming.

Bag. If paper: be careful with money. Cloth: business improving. Leather: a journey. A full bag: wishes will come true.

Bed. If empty: a death omen (perhaps for another). Yourself in a strange bed: business improving. Your own bed: security.

Bells. One bell ringing: bad news. Many bells: good news. Church bells: be wary of others.

Blood. Yours, spilled: trouble coming, perhaps at home. Having a transfusion: problems will be overcome.

Bones. Of animals or cooked meat: financial losses. Human: an inheritance. Fish: an illness.

Bridge. If intact: a change will bring good fortune. If damaged: avoid changes for a while.

Cage. If empty: setbacks in love. Containing birds: happiness in love.

Car. If speeding: news will arrive. If in an accident: a happy discovery. If broken down: be wary of a loved one.

Cave. An ill omen – unless you find your way out, signifying troubles overcome.

Cemetery. Visiting one: prosperity. A well-tended cemetery: happiness coming. An unkempt one: trouble coming.

Clock. A warning against time-wasting. Hearing one strike: happiness coming. A stopped clock: omen of health.

Colours. Red: high negative emotion (anger). Blue: help from others. Black: an ill omen. White: success. Yellow: setbacks.

Elopement – omen of disappointment, heartbreak

Orange: delays. Green: travel (or news). Brown: money coming. (Colours can be useful adjuncts to fill out interpretations of other images.)

Cooking. Good omen of prosperity and well-being.

Death. Your own: improved health or wealth. Another's: a birth or other happy event.

Doll. Good omen of happiness at home.

Door. Open: an opportunity lost. Closed: wishes may come true. Many doors: many possibilities opening up.

Eating. If yourself alone: quarrels and setbacks. If with others: a good omen. Over-eating: good news.

Examination. If you do badly: omen of failure. Success if you do well.

Jungle – beware financial or romantic 'tangles'

Lap – a love affair in the offing

Feet. Bare: a new romance. Washing: omen of sadness. Sore: trouble coming. Itchy: enjoyable travel.

Fire. An ill omen. House on fire: someone needs your help. Putting out a fire: achievement. Being burned: trouble ahead. Firemen: good news.

Flood. Omen of trouble; short lived if the water is clear. Being swept away: unhappiness in love.

Friend. Omen of happiness. A new friend: something lost will be found. A distant friend: news will come. Quarrelling with friends: a minor illness.

Funeral. Omen of happiness. Your own: present troubles are ending.

Garden. Good omen if neat and well kept, ill if neglected.

Log – good omen in most forms

Ghost. Good omen. If it speaks: a temptation to be resisted, or an illness.

Glass. Good omen if clean, bad if dirty. Cleaning glass: go carefully. Broken glass: troubles ahead.

Gold. An ill omen. Prospecting for gold: a change for the better.

Guns. Harm will be done to you. Loading a gun: be careful of your temper.

Hair. Prosperity ahead. Combing or brushing: a problem will be overcome. Hair-cut: success. Setting hair: good luck in love. Thinning hair: trouble ahead.

Hat. New: good omen. Old or dirty: setbacks. Lost: money worries. Unusual: social success. Ill-fitting: disappointment.

House. Buying: a romance. Selling: an end to worry. Building: unexpected money coming. Empty or derelict: sadness, loss. Old: a happy reunion. New: security.

Illness. Yourself: problems to confront. Others: you will be let down.

Injury. To yourself: beware of enemies. To your reputation: promotion or honours to come.

Jewellery. Good omen generally. Diamonds: losses. Pearls: good luck. Emeralds: separation, loss. Sapphires: a warning. Rubies: a love affair.

Maid – ill omen unless you actually have one

Judge. Difficulties and setbacks coming.

Keys. Found: a good omen. Lost: bad luck. Broken: a chance lost. Given: happiness. Received: help from others.

Kitchen. Social pleasure and good health, if clean. If untidy: illness.

Knife. Sharp: quarrels. Dull: a struggle. Broken: setbacks in love. Rusty or dirty: domestic trouble. Open penknife: legal difficulties. Closed: money troubles. Being cut by: be careful of debt.

Letter. If good news: a good omen. Business letter: be careful with money. Mailing a letter: a good omen.

Lightning. A very good omen. With thunder: worries will give way to happiness.

Millionaire – financial improvements on their way

Mud – excellent omen of good fortune

Logs. A good omen. Sawing: domestic happiness. Log cabin: peace and contentment.

Lottery. Win or lose, an omen of domestic strife.

Map. Omen of travel or change. Large: a long journey. Coloured: travel will bring benefits. Drawing a map: good luck.

Mask. If on yourself: financial gain. On others: beware of deceit.

Mirror. To see yourself: beware of deceit. Others: disloyal friends. Broken: disaster.

Money. Getting or spending: a good omen either way. Losing: unexpected gain. Finding: disappointment. Stealing: good luck. Borrowing: bad luck.

Moon. Full: happiness in love. New: success in business. Bright: happiness and prosperity. Obscured: ill health.

Nose – if sore or hurt, omen of prosperity

Music. A very good omen – unless discordant, which warns of setbacks and treachery.

Name. To forget your own: be careful of prospective arrangements. To forget another's: the same. Others forgetting yours: personal troubles.

Newspaper. Reading: good news coming. Buying: your position will improve. As wrapping: a joyous reunion.

Nuts. Eating: good health. Cracking: success. Rotten: beware enemies.

Occultism. In any form, a valuable secret to be learned.

Oil. Drilling for: success. Oiling machinery: achievement. On yourself: troubles are ending. Cooking with: an enemy.

Operation. If on yourself: a change for the better. On another: unexpected news.

Orchard. A very good omen if in fruit. In bloom: good luck. Neglected: a setback.

Parents. Father: success in business. Mother: happiness in love. Death of either: sad news, ill luck.

Party. If yours: a bad omen. If another's: good luck. High society: ill luck. Wild party: beware scandal.

Piano. If you were playing: success. If another: good luck. Moving one: a promotion. Out of tune: setbacks.

Poison. Taking it: be cautious and firm. Others taking: triumph over obstacles. Giving it: setbacks in love, betrayal.

Prison. Yourself inside: a bad omen. Release or escape: bad times ending. Others inside: success in business.

Queue. Standing in: useful advice or gifts to come.

Rabbi. If you are Jewish: prosperity coming. If not: help coming from friends.

Rain. Difficulties, small ones if only a drizzle. Being caught in: unexpected gain. Leaking roof: betrayal.

Officer – police, money troubles; army, security

Restaurant. Visiting with family: a good omen. With a lover: financial setbacks. Expensive: money worries.

Ring. Losing: good omen, mostly financial. Finding: a new romance or friendship. Receiving: the same as finding.

River. Clear: a good omen. Murky: bad omen. Falling in: domestic troubles. Jumping in: go carefully. On the bank: success ahead.

Rope. Coiled or coiling: hardships have been overcome. Uncoiling: beneficial change. A noose: a trap, or love entanglement. Making rope: a problem solved. Walking a tightrope: profit from speculation.

Running. If towards a goal: ambition fulfilled. Aimless: ambition frustrated. In fear: security. In pursuit: good luck.

Salt. A good omen. Spilled: temporary setback.

Sand. Be wary of a new friend.

Party – yours, a warning; another's, good luck

Piano – success, whether playing or listening

School. Financial gain. Being in: delays and setbacks from past associations. Leaving: good luck.

Scream. Your own: good omen. Others': bad news coming.

Sea. Voyage: a problem overcome. Swimming: opportunity coming. Falling in: beware jealous friends. Calm sea: good luck. Stormy: a bad omen.

Sex. Having intercourse enjoyably: a good omen, personal happiness. Watching others: an ill omen. A sex change: unexpected change for the better domestically.

Sex organs. If sound and intact: a good omen of success and prosperity. If ill-formed or diseased: setbacks and difficulties. If none at all: worries, a sense of inadequacy.

Ship. Good omen for business. A model: a new romance. A wreck: beware of gossip about you.

Shoes. New: beware of overconfidence. Old and worn:

success. Lost: make some changes in your life. Shining: unexpected good luck.

Sky. If clear: a good omen. Cloudy: an ill omen if heavily clouded, omen of aid from others if mildly overcast. Red sky: money coming. Rainbow: ill luck.

Sun. A good omen if bright and warm. Sunset: an ill omen if especially lovely. Through clouds: troubles will end soon. Red sun: conflict ahead.

Telephone. Yourself using: good luck in business. Being telephoned: a setback. Out of order: bad news on the way.

Television. If enjoyable: progress being made. If dull or upsetting: beware external influences. Out of order: difficulties.

Traffic. A jam: obstacles. Smooth-flowing: problems of a domestic nature being overcome. Accident: losses.

Plank – use extra caution

Royalty – excellent omen of good fortune

Tramp. Yourself as: progress being made. Helping one: promotion, advancement. Refusing help: setbacks, disappointments.

Treasure. Finding: prosperity. Digging for: good health. Diving for: a gift or inheritance.

Tunnel. Passing through: an opportunity coming. Railway tunnel: beware enemies. Lost in one: ill luck.

Umbrella. Good omen of security. Broken or torn: setbacks coming.

Uniforms. Promotion and success for a man; happiness in love and marriage for a woman.

Vegetables. Eating: setbacks and obstacles. Growing: domestic happiness. Serving: slow progress. Rotten: more setbacks.

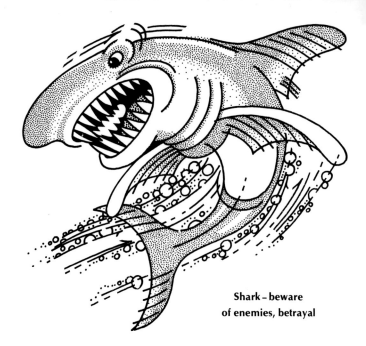

**Shark – beware
of enemies, betrayal**

Visitor. Being one: beware deceit and disloyalty. Receiving one: rethink present plans.

Wagon. Loaded: financial gain. Riding one: be careful about money. Hay wagon: a good omen.

Water. Calm: a good omen, as is clear. Rough or murky: ill omen. Running water: happiness. Waterfall: prosperity, advancement. Drinking: good luck. Spilling: curb your temper. Hot water: setbacks in business.

Wedding. Happiness; sometimes shortlived.

Wind. Storm: adversity, disappointment. Strong wind: minor obstacles. Breeze: a good omen.

Window. Opened: success. Closed: a threat will be averted. Broken: a change coming. Climbing or jumping from: unexpected luck. Climbing in: opportunity coming.

Yawn. Obstacles ahead, some of your own making.

Zoo. Good omen. Visiting with children: travel, good luck. With a lover: setbacks.

Extending the Omens

Catalogues of that sort can take you quite a long way towards reasonably enjoyable and adequate interpretation. But there are other techniques that can help to refine and develop your skill – among them the common distinction made by experts between 'true' dreams and 'meaningless' dreams.

The latter do not well up so much from the depths of the unconscious as from more superficial stimuli. These might

Snake – troubles and difficulties ahead; treachery

Teeth – having good teeth is a good omen (as is dentistry)

be digestive upsets (which tend to happen early in sleep); external effects like cold or discomfort or disturbing noises; unusual states of mind like tension, overexcitement, depression, anxiety. So if you have a dream of a sudden, frightening noise, and wake up to find that you have been disturbed by an unsilenced motorcycle out on the street, the dream can be ignored. (But if you dream of a loud noise when there is no outer stimulus, it is an omen of domestic upsets.)

Similarly, if you are worried about your son, say, and have an unnerving dream about him, the dream is useless for fortune telling – because it merely echoes your anxiety. And if you dream about something that is commonplace to you in your everyday life, that too is of no use. Your dream of a hospital, say, would be a warning to change your way of life – unless you are a doctor, nurse, orderly or the like, in which case it is just another 'echo' dream which should not be interpreted.

Once you have established that the dream comes from the proper regions of the soundly sleeping and undisturbed mind, you can still do more for interpretation than merely reeling off the meaning from the catalogue. Take a leaf from the psychoanalyst's book and ask the dreamer for his or her own *associations* with the images. Does that grandfather

War – quarrels and difficulties coming

clock, or fast-speeding train, or ruined church, have any special meaning in the dreamer's life? Noting personalised connections like these, and letting the intuition – as always – play over them, can give your interpretations valuable new dimensions.

Also, take care to note *all* the images in a dream. If the dreamer saw himself riding in a fast sports car on a winding mountain road under a heavily overcast sky, follow up all these images. And inquire after others: the colour of the car, the nature of the driver, the other passengers, the rest of the landscape. All these might produce a bewildering array of disconnected or even contradictory meanings; but they are at least as likely to open out and clarify the overall meaning of the dream.

Be careful, though, not to press the dreamer *too* hard for further details, or he may start, unknowingly, to invent them. Here is the main trouble with dreams: they are unconscious events, glimpsed only fragmentarily, if at all, by the conscious mind, and so are annoyingly elusive in the conscious memory. How often have you had a striking dream of which every single detail – except the awareness that you had dreamed – vanished from your memory by midday?

The secret is to induce a dreamer who wishes to have his or her dreams interpreted to keep pad and pencil close to the bedside. Immediately upon awakening, the dreamer must scribble at high speed everything that can be recalled about the dream before it fades – concentrating on resisting the temptation to edit and embellish. It can help, too, if at the same time the immediate associations with the dream images that come to mind are jotted down, for these 'free', unsummoned associations can be the most telling of all.

As you gain experience, you will of course become aware

of patterns and tendencies within the images: note, for instance, how often there are double meanings in image and omen, as when being 'swept away' by a flood is an omen of a new love affair. You may also spend some time profitably looking into the writings of Freud and Jung on the general patterns and shapes of dreams. Freud's awareness of recurring elements — like symbols of sexual obsession or repression, symbols of wish fulfilment and the other 'complexes' we associate with his discoveries – can give you valuable insights. And Jung, too, can be instructive, with his studies of 'compensating' dreams (the little clerk dreaming of himself as Napoleon) and much more. Jung it was, too, who uncovered the vital importance of the mighty 'archetypal' image patterns that take many forms, in myth as well as dream, but that lurk within the depths of each of us — symbols like the hero figure, the conflict with monsters, the mother goddess, or magically powerful shapes like the cross and the circle.

All these extra elements can make the difference between an obvious, one-dimensional statement of the stereotyped meanings and an individualised reading of a dream. Again, we come back to intuition, imaginative insight, the 'feeling' for the right interpretation to fit the case.

And this ability will help you avoid, as you must, damaging any of your subjects who suffer from that suggestibility mentioned before. Many dream images are threatening and distressing, and so are their omens: no one likes to know that his or her own mind has thrown up an advance warning of disaster or even death — especially not while they may still be a little shaky from the impact of the dream itself. Personalised and intuitively adjusted interpretation can take the curse off such omens, and can save the dreamer from, at the least, a nagging if subliminal anxiety.

Steps Across Time

Part of the reason why people can be unnerved by their more dire dreams comes from the considerable body of well-authenticated cases of dreams that contained direct, explicit *foreknowledge*. History is full of instances of such 'precognition': Abraham Lincoln dreaming accurately of his own assassination and 'lying in state'; an Austrian bishop who dreamed of the killing of Archduke Ferdinand, in 1914, which launched the First World War; an English nobleman who dreamed on two successive nights that the *Titanic* would sink, and so wisely cancelling the passage he had booked on its ill-fated sailing; Adolf Hitler, when a common soldier in the First World War, dreaming that his trench would collapse, and so escaping death when it actually did; or the woman who rang the White House in 1963 to warn President John F. Kennedy not to go to Dallas, for she had dreamed he would die there.

Precognition, and its corollary from the waking state, clairvoyance, have come in for much rigorous scientific study in recent years. Commentators of the stature and wisdom of Arthur Koestler, J. B. Priestley and Brian Inglis will all assure us that only the most blinkered set of rationalist prejudices will still insist that 'extrasensory perception' is nonsense. So it may be that in the course of fortune telling by dreams, some of your subjects – or you yourself – may find that one of those hastily scribbled early-morning notes of a dream may turn out to be a fairly accurate prediction of a later happening. (Not all precognitive dreams, by any means, concern portentous events like death and disaster. At least as many well-attested cases relate to extremely normal, even trivial events in the dreamer's life.)

If such a thing does happen, you might inform the Society for Psychical Research or some similar professional and reputable body which collects such instances. Otherwise, such dreams will be of little use to you for fortune telling – until such time as science discovers, if it ever does, how these glimpses across time (and space) happen. When that discovery is made, it may turn out that some sort of ESP faculty exists in all of us. It may also be that some people will learn to switch it on and off, at will. At that point, all the fortune tellers and seers in the world will be put out of business.

But meanwhile, we have only the centuries of fortune-telling tradition, the libraries full of writings on divination and the hoped-for qualities of our own intuitions to fall back on, for glimpses of what is to come. Personally I have no doubt that the full and proper exercise of the intuitive ability – with all its emotive, subjective, 'non-rational' but very real perceptual value – goes a long way towards taking us into the shadow-land of extrasensory perception. I also feel sure that some intuitive sense is part of the normal equipment of every human being, part of our humanness – which is why, potentially, anyone might learn to tell fortunes. Like muscles or memories, it needs constant use to be developed, and it needs to be used trustingly and confidently to be used properly. But without it, no matter how many 'meanings' and 'systems' you have committed to memory, you will never get past the learner stage as a fortune teller.

Index

Figures in bold refer to illustrations

Acknowledgments

The painting on page 64 is the copyright of S.P.A.D.E.M., Paris, 1978. The edition of *Raphael's Astronomical Ephemeris of the Planets' Places for 1949* illustrated on page 27 is published by W. Foulsham & Co. Ltd., Slough; the third edition of *I Ching or Book of Changes*, illustrated on page 129, is translated by Richard Wilhelm and published by Routledge and Kegan Paul, London. Ron Hayward drew the illustrations for the chapter on palmistry, Russell Coulson the cartoons for the chapter on dreams.

Photographs
Animal Graphics, Crawley 59 bottom; Mary Evans Picture Library, London 57, 61; Photographie Giraudon, Paris 50; Gulbenkian Foundation, Lisbon 60 bottom; Hamlyn Group Picture Library 50, 52, 59 top, 62; Commander H. R. Hatfield, Sevenoaks 122; Michael Holford Library, Loughton 60 top left; Eric Hosking, London 60 top right; Los Alamos Scientific Laboratory, New Mexico (Bill Jack Rodgers) 58 top; National Gallery, London 63; Tony Stone Associates, London 58 below left and right; Tate Gallery, London 64.